What Others Are Saying About Paul Heys and This Book

"I know Paul better than I know Warren Buffet, but I know them both well enough to see tremendous similarities in their investment style. Both have a tremendous grasp of the importance "temperament" plays in an investor's success. They both know how to take advantage of the investment opportunities that are created when emotion and mass hysteria infect the investment markets from time to time."

—**David Cohn, Former Regent, University of Washington**

"I want to express my admiration for what Paul has achieved in this book. It makes a significant and unique contribution that is destined to have a major impact on the wealth accumulation of many people. The psychological concepts that influence wealth-related decisions and behaviors for better or worse are clearly presented and the scientific basis made clear. The mental and emotional landmines that can sabotage financial decision making are presented in an engaging and understandable manner, emphasizing how "normal" their influences are in our lives.

This book is not pop psychology; rather, it is informed by a solid scientific base. I believe it has the potential to become a best seller. "

—**Ronald E. Smith, PhD, Psychology Professor, University of Washington, Former Director, UW Clinical Psychology Program**

"This book manages to take the research on financial decision making and translate it into understandable and workable advice for general public. It also emphasizes that building financial wealth gives us the freedom to build non-financial wealth. Few investment books mention that 'Mere financial capital (money) doesn't make a person wealthy.' This book does."

—**Pam Whalley, Director, Center for Economic and Financial Education, Western Washington University**

"Warren Buffet says to be a success, "You only have to do a very few things right in your life so long as you don't do too many things wrong." Paul's book does a wonderful job of helping us understand the few most important financial decisions we must get right, as well as showing how to protect ourselves from the worst impulses that tend to sink our financial ship. And if that isn't reason enough to get this book, consider that the book's Appendix E contains a brilliantly written summary by Erik Johnson of Nobel laureate Daniel Kahneman's 500 page masterpiece, *Thinking, Fast and Slow*."

—Paul Merriman, Financial Contributor: *MarketWatch*,
Chairman: Merriman Financial Education Foundation

"Kudos to Paul Heys for this wise and lucid guide to financial and psychological wealth. By applying and simplifying economic and cognitive science, he shows us the path to both fiscal fitness and human flourishing."

—David Myers, Ph.D, Psychology Professor, Hope College,
Co-Author: *Psychology, 12th Edition*

"Paul has guided our financial affairs for the past 46years. His steady hand on the controls of our investments has enabled us to touchdown smoothly at our financial destination. We might have made it without him, but it wouldn't have been as smooth a flight, as short a trip, or as enjoyable a ride. He is a man of rare intellect and real integrity, and the world's greatest financial co-pilot."

—Clint Viebrock, Captain, Retired, Delta Airlines

"Paul Heys knows the meaning of true wealth. His new *Spending Your Way to Wealth* is a generous gift to future generations about how to prioritize experiences and relationships over wealth while using money to enrich our lives. Too many people chase after dollars without knowing what those dollars can actually do for them. Use Paul's book as your personal compass as he sets the record straight with satisfying, long-lasting results."

—Patrick Snow, International Bestselling Author of
Creating Your Own Destiny **and** *The Affluent Entrepreneur*

"Paul Heys' new book, *Spending Your Way to Wealth*, is a revolutionary look at what it means to be wealthy. Heys teaches people how to stop wasteful spending and invest their money in appreciating assets. This book should be recommended reading for everyone."

—Robert Cannon, Financial Services Professional, New York Life

"This book is the perfect graduation gift for the high school or college student. It encompasses everything they don't teach in school that you need to know to truly succeed in life."

—David Sievers, Life Coach and Author: *Flowing Through Change*

"Paul and I served together in the Air Force Reserve where I first observed his unique training ability and style. The training skills he once utilized to assure that flight crews were safe, proficient and qualified, he today employs to help people reach their financial destination safely, comfortably and with confidence. I know, because he helped "train" me, and has guided my financial ship for the past 47 years."

—Dave Covey, Colonel, USAFR

"I wish someone had given me this book when I was younger. It would have directed my spending and investing in ways that would have made me re-think my career, relationships, and what I truly wanted out of life. I am grateful I have it now for financial guidance and easy reference. *Spending Your Way to Wealth* is the kind of book that changes lives."

—Tyler R. Tichelaar, Ph.D., Author: *Narrow Lives* **and** *The Best Place*

"*Spending Your Way to Wealth* is far more than an eye-catching title. It is a groundbreaking exploration of behavioral finance. Young and old, personal and professional, novice and seasoned financial player alike can make their way through this book without ever feeling like they are lost. This book places ever-present issues in our everyday lives in a new light and gives us an opportunity to evaluate our ideas about wealth, value, and our personal relationship to these concepts."

—Robert Band, CPA, CEO, and author of *Turning Profits into Fortunes*

SPENDING YOUR WAY
to WEALTH

SPENDING YOUR WAY *to* WEALTH

Setting Your Compass Course to Steer in the Direction of True Wealth

Paul Heys

KITSAP
PUBLISHING

KITSAP PUBLISHING

& Investorship Publishing

Spending Your Way to Wealth
First edition, published 2020
Copyright © 2020, Paul Heys

By Paul M. Heys and John Parsons

Cover Design and Interior Layout by Reprospace, LLC
Cartoons by Erik Johnson
Summary of *Thinking, Fast and Slow* used with permission. Copyright © 2019, Erik Johnson

Hardcover ISBN-13: 978-1-942661-25-2
Paperback ISBN-13: 978-1-952685-03-3

This book contains information about financial firms and their products and services such as real estate, stocks, bonds, and other types of investments. While this book is intended to provide information on financial matters and investments, such information or references should not be construed or interpreted as investment advice or viewed as an endorsement. The author has invested and likely will invest in the products and services discussed in this book. However, any comments or suggestions offered in this book regarding such financial firms or their products and services are solely the opinions of the author.

This book utilizes several assumptions on which to base likely future financial outcomes. During the past 5+ decades, the U.S. economy has experienced a yearly inflation rate that has averaged about 3% per year. Likewise, while the value of major American-based companies has also varied from year to year, one of the most common benchmarks for such companies' growth is tracked by Standard & Poors Inc. and reported as the S&P 500 Stock Index. This index has shown an average growth rate of approximately 10% per year over the past five decades. While there can be no assurance that either the U.S. inflation rate or the S&P 500 Stock Index will experience the same average rate in the future that it has in the past, the duration of time over which the averages have been calculated provides a basis for an assumption of its continuance in the future.

20200612

Published by Kitsap Publishing
P.O. Box 572
Poulsbo, WA 98370
www.KitsapPublishing.com in cooperation with Investorship Publishing

Dedication

This book is dedicated to the many committed educators whose daily efforts are focused on helping us learn new things on which to base our future decisions. Whether teaching a young kindergarten child to be nice, kind and considerate, or teaching a seasoned astronaut how to react to outer space, there can be no greater professional challenge than helping to shape to prepare our minds for the future.

To my parents who taught me to play hard, think always, and be kind. I'm not sure where you're listening from, but I know you hear me. To my darling wife Linda, without whose support life could not be so wonderful; "I treasure you". To my dear and wonderful sons, Captain Michael and Captain Graeme, you have been among my best educators; having taught me how wonderful it is to be proud. May the stars that guide your ships of life stay bright, beautiful and ever present; and may your cruise to your ultimate Snug Harbor be joyous.

Acknowledgments

Wealth is defined in both monetary and non-monetary ways. The latter includes integrity, wisdom, commitment, great memories, and more. No book about the psychology of wealth(s) and spending would be possible without the input of those who have an abundance of such wealths.

It's impossible to thank everyone who contributed facts, knowledge, and wisdom to this book, or who have encouraged me to write it. But I would like to acknowledge some of those whose generosity of wealth have inspired its writing. They have been instrumental in helping cultivate, activate, and stimulate both the human mind and spirit.

Since this work is a practical application of the bestselling book, *Thinking, Fast and Slow,* I would like to thank its author and Nobel laureate, Daniel Kahneman. His research and study of the human mind and its cognitive abilities and limitations have helped shape today's understanding of decision making. Without his profound work, this book would not be possible.

Thanks also to another brilliant psychologist and friend, Professor Ronald E. Smith. Ron generously allocated much of his time, knowledge, and expertise to collaborate with me in developing a financial philosophy we termed "Investorship". Admittedly a new word, it is an adjective that describes the thinking and skills common to successful financial decision makers like Warren Buffett, John Bogle, and Sir John Templeton.

I have also benefited greatly from my time with renowned psychologists David Myers and Meir Statman—authors of many books on the human mind and its capabilities and limitations when dealing with monetary and non-monetary environments.

Another individual, without whom this book probably would have never progressed beyond my own mind, is my co-writer, John Parsons. John came into my life following a national search for someone with experience in book creation and thinking skills that could help me transform 50+ years of financial advising experience into a book that could enable people cope more effectively with the challenges of wealth creation and preservation. John has become not only a dear friend but an extremely knowledgeable and trusted source of content.

The director of Western Washington University's Center for Economic and Financial Education, Pamela Whalley, has also helped me greatly. During her outstanding, multi-decade career, she has guided thousands of professional educators in the development and implementation of financial literacy curricula for a multitude of schools and educational partnerships. Her teaching methods are role models for educators everywhere.

In addition, I have long known and appreciated Paul Merriman for his commitment to the financial education of people of all ages. Paul's career as a financial advisor resulted in the creation of a prominent investment advisory firm bearing his name. Following retirement, he created and funded the Merriman Financial Education Foundation: a non-profit organization committed to furthering public education on sound financial and investing principles. His writings, videos, and podcasts are accessible on www.paulmerriman.com and his articles appear regularly on Dow Jones' website, *MarketWatch*.

Special thanks to Ingemar Anderson, my publisher, Erik Johnson, my cartoonist and fellow student of Daniel Kahneman, Kathryn Brownson, my intrepid editor, and Patrick Snow, marketing strategist. Their enthusiasm for the book, and their conviction that it could become a bestseller, is an author's ultimate compliment.

Other standouts who lent their minds and rolled up their sleeves to help make this book a reality include (in alphabetical order): Sheryl Belt—Curriculum Superintendent of the Bainbridge Island School District, Dan Boyden—Eatonville High School, Allyson Brown—

Executive Director of the Bainbridge School Foundation, Tony and Katie Chace, Carolyn Clarke, Marina Cofer-Wildsmith, Stefan Cordova—Founder of Digitegy Inc., Joanne Croghan, Wendy del Valle, Everett and Bernie DuBois—VP and Treasurer (Retired) at Burlington Resources, Maureen Fitz-Roberts—Rotary Club District Governor, Mike Florian, Ed Gilbert—Executive Director of the Bainbridge Island Land Trust, Christy Givens, Robin Goldson, Arnie and Jenny Gooder, Jim Hopper—Executive Director of the Bainbridge Island Community Foundation, Marty Juergens, John and Chris Kiley, John and Nancy Klimp, Brianna Kosowitz—Executive Director of the Bainbridge Island History Museum, Jim Laws, Tom and Judy Lindsley, Bob and Margret Linz, Ron Loggi—Senior Financial Analyst for the City of Bainbridge Island, Don Mannino, Sherryl McCauly, Zan Merriman, Kelly Muldrow, Sam Parsons, Warren Parsons, Senator Christine Rolfes—Washington State 23rd District, the Rotary Club of Bainbridge Island, Lynn Smith—President of the Bainbridge Island School Board, Gary Sundholm—UW Accounting Professor Emeritus, Clint Viebrock, Nancy Walker, and Windstar Cruise Lines.

Finally, to all the people I've had the privilege of knowing and serving as a financial advisor, thank you for being such brilliant teachers about what is best among us.

Contents

Preface

Read This First!

PART 1

When I began writing this book, the word "Corona" conjured pleasant visions of happy, relaxed people sipping cold, Mexican beers, at parties or on warm, sandy beaches. Our vision of a happy, normal life involved gatherings with family, friends, and co-workers—at restaurants, theaters, a local sporting event, and of course spending money at our favorite shopping mall. It's what *normal* people do (or did).

Today, the word "corona" sends a chill down our collective spine. The new coronavirus, COVID-19, banished our thoughts of warm sand, sunshine, and relaxed social gatherings. The pandemic brought about enormous, often traumatic changes to our way of life. We had to adopt new habits in order to assure basic survival. Instead of thinking about where our next vacation will be, we wondered if our next trip from home might be to the hospital. Daily spending decisions were accompanied by waves of unaccustomed stress and panic. And instead of worrying that our retirement account was less than ideal, we realized it was probably under-funded, and feared that our ability to sustain ourselves later in life might be impossible.

In the past, all too many people consistently spent without taking sufficient time to consider the longer-term consequences of each expenditure. Such consequences include the high likelihood that a huge percentage of the money spent every day *would likely have zero financial value in the future*. However, if that expenditure had been allocated differently, into things with increasing value (financial assets, real estate, savings accounts, etc.), *it could become thousands, hundreds of thousands, and even millions of dollars* during the spender's lifetime. To do so does not require all of us to become Warren Buffett. Rather, it means we just have to make modest changes in how we approach spending. That process, which has always been essential to achieving future financial wealth, has just become far more essential.

Those spending practices, engaged in by so many people in the pre-coronavirus era, prompted the writing of this book. I hoped the book could cause some readers to slow down, modify their spending practices and establish new ones that would enhance their financial futures. My 40 years of experience spent helping to guide people's investment practices has left me keenly aware of an important reality. People are very reluctant and slow to change their habits, unless and until forced to; or until they become sufficiently motivated to do so.

Now, before the book was completed, an event occurred that was so devastating that lives throughout the world have changed forever. The adversity caused by the coronavirus has forced us to abandon our old habits and replace them with survival habits. Hopefully, our discovery that we are all capable of change, and that change can occur quickly and decisively, will be a beneficial legacy of the coronavirus era.

This book is grounded on the premise that no behavior so impacts or influences our financial situation than our spending behavior. Hopefully the new spending habits that we have adopted during the coronavirus era will enable us to return to our prior level of financial normalcy. And, if we retain many of these new spending habits and supplement them with the suggestions, recommendations and tools provided in this book, we can go beyond merely returning to our previous level of financial security, we can achieve heightened levels of financial wealth. We can brighten not only our financial future; we can start to decrease our level of anxiety associated with our financial activity. Additionally, we can find time to invest our time, our energy and ourselves in worthy and productive activities.

May your new spending habits enable you to spend your way to wealths (plural; as in a wealth of happiness, a wealth of success, a wealth of friendships, a wealth of great memories, etc., etc., etc., and, yes; a wealth of sufficient financial assets.) May we all strive to have a diversified portfolio of many wealths.

PART 2

Socrates is credited with having said, "There is no surer sign of a person's education and intellect, than their ability, willingness, and propensity, to set aside their beliefs and convictions, long enough and often enough, to discover new things on which to base them." This book is all about the long-term, positive consequences that can result from setting aside old habits and beliefs long enough to discover the enormous benefits that can result.

The concepts in this book will not be new to many readers. However, just because a concept is familiar does not guarantee it automatically will be put to good use. This is especially true when it comes to how we deal with financial matters.

Seeing the title of this book will lead most to conclude that it is about spending money and achieving financial wealth. That assumption is not altogether wrong, but it overlooks the broader meanings of both *wealth* and *spending*—the central theme and purpose of the book.

Wealth is defined as *an abundance of something of value*. We can have many wealths (plural) besides money. They include a wealth of satisfaction, of friendships, of great memories, and scores of other good things. Since wealth—financial and non-financial—takes so many positive forms, it's right to assume that their pursuit is both worthy and noble. With this book, we hope to explain the worthiness of these many kinds of wealth, to inform the reader on the various ways of acquiring them, and to motivate every reader to pursue, embody, and benefit from them.

Spending, the other key subject of the book, is defined as *the exchange of one thing of perceived value for another thing of greater perceived value.* This requires an ability to consider whether our perception of value results from having a need or a want, and how that influences our motivation to spend. In other words, what motivates us to spend our time, our energy, our knowledge, or our financial assets—money—to meet that need or want?

To add depth to our self-understanding of these ideas, the book draws heavily on the past two decades of scientific research in the areas of brain function and the psychology of thinking—or metacognition. The science-based findings of Princeton psychology professor and Nobel Prize winner Daniel Kahneman are cited throughout the book as examples of how some people are able—and motivated—to achieve greater decision-making skills, with better results than those achieved by most normal people.

When applied to the topics of wealth and spending—broadly defined—these principles will prove invaluable. "Behavioral finance" is a term widely accepted among professional economists and financial professionals but less understood by ordinary people. This book is intended to remedy that situation.

Introduction

It's Never Too Late

*"We cannot solve our problems with the same thinking
we used when we created them."*
— Albert Einstein

In a recent survey by Bankrate.com, 21% of the respondents said they had set aside nothing for retirement, emergencies, and other financial needs. Almost half said they had set aside 10% or less. In 2016, the Federal Reserve reported that a shocking number of Americans (46%) said they would not have enough to cover a $400 emergency expense.

The way we spend explains the reason for these statistics. For example, spending $50 per week on snacks, gadgets, eating out, and so on, may feel satisfying. But there's a huge downside. In 30 years, had that amount been spent differently, it's value would have been over a half million dollars. In 40 years, the number would be over $1.5 million!

This book will help you understand why you make these unfortunate decisions every day. It's quite simple. You are normal. Just ask yourself:

"Have I ever said or done something and,
moments or hours later, wondered why?"

"Have I ever slapped my forehead and exclaimed,
'I did it again!' (probably not out loud)?"

"Have I ever experienced 'buyer's remorse'
after making a decision?"

"Have I ever made a hasty decision involving money
that created strife or hardship?"

If the answer is yes, you are not alone. Reacting to something instead of reflecting on the possible consequences is what humans do. When the results are negative, the pain is real—but not always immediate. The good news is our normal responses can be changed to *normal plus*, especially when it comes to spending and wealth.

In this book, you will learn a lot about yourself and what it means to be normal. You'll also learn surprising things about something we do almost every day (spend money) and the true nature of what we hope to get in return—wealth. This means not only financial wealth but also the many experiences of personal satisfaction and expression that constitute non-financial wealth.

Because this book deals with how we spend and spill our money, it will help you understand the significant difference between price and value, the nature of risk, and especially the need to pause, reflect, and take the long view rather than react to every bump in the financial road. The book will give you a practical strategy for spending that will result in substantial wealth in the long term.

My Own Story

My early career as a U.S. Air Force flight instructor, and later as an FAA-licensed instructor pilot, enabled me to help others plan their financial journey. The flight preparations and routine procedures I taught, in classrooms and cockpits, dealt with planning and rehearsing one's actions. These lessons were comparable to the financial advice and assistance I later gave individuals and institutions as the founding director of a commercial bank and as vice president at the international investment firm Smith Barney. Both provided the necessary steps to assure a safe journey, and a safe arrival at the desired destination.

Before retiring, my principal activities centered on assisting others to make wise and informed investment decisions. I also wrote and spoke on a wide range of subjects, including financial market history, investing practices, investment performance, financial management, and financial planning. The investments I made during my active employment years have been the primary source of my post-retirement income that resulted from the application of the principles described in this book.

My post-retirement work has been driven by an acute interest in how people make financial decisions. I collaborated with Ronald E. Smith, psychology professor at the University of Washington. We researched and wrote on the subject of behavioral finance and conducted workshops which were designed to enlighten the participants on how their thinking and behavior impacted the results of their financial decisions.

We focused on the pioneering work by noted psychologists Daniel Kahneman (professor emeritus at Princeton University) and Amos Tversky (former psychology professor at Stanford). Their scientific research and findings of fact led to the creation of the field of behavioral economics, also known as "behavioral finance." Their work led to Professor Kahneman's 2002 Nobel Prize in economics—and the basis of his best-selling 2011 book, *Thinking, Fast and Slow*.

This book is intended to inspire readers to become more aware of Professor Kahneman's and others' ground-breaking discoveries regarding people's thinking and behavior—specifically, how thinking and behavior affect the outcome of a person's financial decisions, and it explains why some very normal people achieve sub-optimal results, while others (referred to in this book as normal plus) are able to achieve so much more.

I don't claim to have all the answers. However, during the span of many decades, I have had the opportunity to work personally with thousands of people as an advisor, educator, and trainer.

Most people I encountered had achieved some level of success in their lives. Some were probably smarter than others. Some were likely better informed, and some were undoubtedly luckier than others. Most considered themselves to be good thinkers and thought of themselves as capable decision makers. They tended to be confident that their choices were likely to meet with success. In spite of their many differences, they were essentially all quite normal.

Occasionally I would encounter a person who differed from most of these other normal people. They tended to possess a great understanding of certain concepts and were content to be less knowledgeable (often ignorant) of many other areas. They were more inclined to acknowledge what they did not know, and often preferred to remain that way; choosing instead to rely on others who possessed the knowledge they lacked. They seemed to exhibit an inner confidence (about themselves and their surroundings) and tended to rely on many of the lessons of history to support their inner confidence.

The characteristic of people in this small segment of the much large group of normal people, I came to describe as *normal plus*. They consistently made financial decisions that produced optimal (significantly better) results as compared with the sub-optimal results achieved by normal people.

The primary goal of this book is, therefore, to help the reader transition from "normal" to *normal plus*.

It's Never Too Late

Two of the most common responses I hear when speaking on this subject are along these lines:

> "That sounds great. Maybe I'll do
> something about it someday."

> "That sounds great, but I've waited too
> long. It's too late for me to invest."

Both responses are completely normal and incorrect—simultaneously! As you will discover, our natural first reaction to an unfamiliar concept is to avoid it and continue doing familiar things, even if we know or suspect the negative results. Likewise, regret over past decisions can prevent us from slowing down and reflecting on the possibilities.

Fortunately, it is never too late to apply these principles, and break through the normal, very human habits that prevent us from "spending our way to wealth." No matter what your situation may be, it is very possible to expand your comfort zone and look at spending and wealth in an entirely new way. Through this book, it would be my great honor to guide you in that journey.

Paul Heys

Foreword

About Investorship

In the late 1990s, Paul Heys and I embarked on a program we dubbed Investorship Training—a melding of his expertise as a financial specialist and mine as a personality psychologist. It was an early example of the principles of behavioral finance, a movement that later won Daniel Kahneman (2002) and Robert Schiller (2013) the Nobel Prize.

Our workshops explored the myriad ways in which social cognitive personality theory—and the psychology of self-regulation—could contribute to a financial education program. These practical, scientifically solid, and personally engaging events were incredibly well received by our audiences. Now, some twenty years later, Paul has achieved a quantum leap forward from our original efforts with his concise, practical, and accessible new book, *Spending Your Way to Wealth*.

This short work demystifies the complex and (to many) daunting principles and facts that experts have come to embrace as behavioral finance. The psychological concepts that influence wealth-related decisions and behaviors—for better or worse—are clearly presented and the scientific basis made clear. The mental and emotional landmines that can sabotage financial decision making are presented in an engaging and understandable manner, emphasizing how "normal" are their influences in our lives.

Beyond that, the book provides behavioral guidelines for rational decision making that require conscious and unconscious awareness of the factors that influence wealth accumulation, on the one hand,

and self-defeating "money spilling," on the other. As the director of a clinical science doctoral program, this exemplifies, purely and simply, "evidence-based practice" of the highest order. This is not pop psychology; rather, it is informed by a solid scientific base.

As the author of more than 20 books, I have learned what works and what doesn't in terms of capturing and influencing readers. This book achieves those goals far better than most "ivory tower" products. It is a book directed at the average reader including those as young as high school students as well as older, experienced adults.

Paul's work makes a significant and unique contribution to the marketplace and is destined to have a major impact on the wealth accumulation of many people.

This is a book that everyone should read, regardless of age or financial situation. It is a brilliant reframing of the psychological concepts that influence wealth-related decisions—told in a clear, engaging, and down-to-earth style. This eminently understandable book will occupy its own niche among the many behavioral finance books on the market today.

Ronald E Smith

Ronald Smith is a psychology professor and former Director of the Clinical Psychology Training Program at the University of Washington. His interests include personality, stress and coping; cognitive-affective coping skills training; and clinical personality assessment. His major research interests are in personality, the study of anxiety, stress and coping, and in performance-enhancement research and interventions.

"Good news; you're normal."

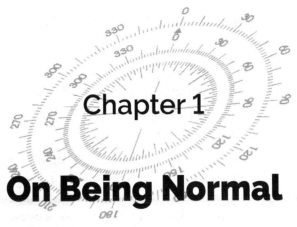

Chapter 1

On Being Normal

*"Is being normal, being ordinary, really such a bad thing?
Is it something inferior? Or, in truth, isn't everybody normal?"*
— Ichiro Kishimi

For most of us, life involves routine. There are high and low points, but a large portion of everyday life is familiar, ordinary, often habitual. In other words, it is normal.

As humans, we exhibit similar, predictable responses to everyday situations. These can be correct and beneficial. Driving a car (after we've learned how) or looking both ways before crossing the street are good examples. We do these things automatically, without giving it much conscious thought. It is what normal people do. Regrettably, we all too often exhibit similar, predictable responses to everyday situations that have very costly consequences, depriving of us of future wealth.

To gauge how normal you are, take a few moments to answer these five questions. Try to answer quickly, without checking the correct answers (in the back of the book) before finishing all five. Write down your answers if you wish.

1. The total cost of a bat and a ball is $1.10. The bat costs $1 more than the ball. How much does the ball cost?
2. Mary's father has five daughters. The names of the first four daughters are: **Nana, Nene, Nini**, and **Nono**. What's the name of the fifth daughter?

3. You are a participant in a race on a straight track. You overtake the second person. What position are you in?

4. You overtake the last person in the same race. What position are you in?

5. A person who cannot speak goes into a shop to buy a toothbrush. By imitating the action of brushing his teeth, he successfully expresses his need to the shopkeeper and makes the purchase. Then, a person who is blind comes into the same shop to buy a pair of protective sunglasses. How does she indicate to the shopkeeper what she wants to buy?

After you finish, check your answers against those printed at the back of the book. If you're like many, you gave answers that instinctively felt true but were in fact incorrect. (You may also find that if you did not answer quickly—contrary to instructions—you probably had more answers correct.) Don't be frustrated. Giving intuitive-but-wrong answers just means you're normal. It also means you're a perfect fit for this book!

Being Normal with Money

Being normal, and responding normally, does not guarantee being right. The easy, intuitive answer can often be the wrong one—based on popular ideas, like the (mostly) ancient belief in a flat earth, or more subtle factors. As humans, we see patterns where none exist, and assign causes to events we don't fully understand. As H. L. Mencken once said, "There is always a well-known solution to every human problem—neat, plausible, and wrong."

Being intuitive-but-wrong is especially true when it comes to money. Ordinary spending choices can have negative consequences—sometimes even dangerous ones. The problem is we make these choices automatically, from unconscious habit. We believe in the value of what we get in return for our spending, but we fail to recognize what we will likely forfeit in the long term.

Acting against our own financial interest does not mean we are unintelligent or irrational. It just means we are normal: thinking and responding *Reactively* rather than *Reflectively*. (More on that in Chapter 2.) We are certainly not alone. To quote the fictional pop philosopher, Walt Kelly's Pogo, "We have met the enemy, and he is us."

Becoming Normal PLUS

As this book will show, being normal is not sufficient when it comes to spending and wealth. Instead, we hope the reader will come to understand the importance of becoming *normal plus*. The book will provide the reader with the information, insights, and incentive to adopt a spending philosophy comparable to that of Warren Buffett and other widely recognized, financially successful individuals.

Anyone who studies the thinking and behavioral characteristics of such financial decision makers will discover striking similarities. Most possess a high level of self-awareness. Most tend to possess core competencies and tend to be steadfast in their adherence to essential disciplines. Most also have the ability to take a long-term approach and not be unduly worried about short-term noise. While outwardly quite normal, they are what is described in this book as *normal plus*. They subscribe to a core philosophy that separates them from most normal people. It is a philosophy this book describes as *Investorship*—a new word that describes a worthy and desirable financial spending practice. It's a philosophy that has enabled countless people to literally spend their way to wealth.

The Investorship spending philosophy is free to anyone with the intellectual and emotional resources to understand its importance and adopt it. Hopefully, that will be you.

This book is about spending and investing, and how normal human behavior can help or hinder our success in accumulating wealth. These ideas have been advanced by Nobel laureate Daniel Kahneman and others under the impressive heading of behavioral finance.

There are other books—long ones—on this subject. However, they are written for advanced readers. This book is intended for existing investors and non-investors—younger adults and others who avoid financial planning as too complicated or scary, as well as older adults who feel it's now too late to start investing. It is also aimed at those who are already investing to a small degree—perhaps through a 401(k) or similar program—but who are unhappy or frustrated in their progress towards greater wealth.

Most of all, the book is intended for those who believe investing is too arcane for them, when it is actually something a financial newcomer can master. My goal is to help you understand the consequences of spending and investment decisions—whether they be the small, incremental ones, or the large major ones. By slowing down and reflecting on these consequences, rather than acting reactively or "intuitively," you will be on a path to spending your way to wealth.

Special Note

While the mathematical calculations utilized in this book are straightforward and uncomplicated, a brief explanation will aid you in better understanding them:

When the book discusses current and future expenses associated with a particular item, it automatically adjusts each future year's expenditure for that item by an estimated inflation factor (3%). Thus, something which costs $1.00 today will cost $1.03 next year, $1.061 the following year, and so on.

Similarly, when the book discusses the possible future value of an investment of $1.00 in an S&P 500 Index fund (which has historically returned an average of 10% per year over an extended period of time), it shows the value of the invested $1.00 will likely be worth $1.10, the following year, $1.21 the following year, and so on.

The calculations in the book were derived from future-value tables similar to those used for the online Investorship calculator. They have been checked for accuracy by significantly credentialed individuals (accountants and financial consultants) whose calculation methodology may differ slightly based on minor formulation differences.

American consumers (people like us) are among the greatest financial spenders in the world. Certainly, we are among the most practiced. We spend more frequently, on more things, in larger amounts and in greater quantities than almost anyone else on earth. Regrettably, most of this spending is at the expense of spending on our future financial security. Since this problem tends not to manifest itself immediately, the magnitude of the problem increases each year until, it ultimately may be unmanageable.

The purpose of this book is to help the reader understand the problems that arise out of spending unchecked by reflection on long-term consequences, and to modify their spending practices in ways that make their future spending the cause of financial wealth.

This book is not intended to deprive us of the pleasure and satisfaction of spending. Rather, its purpose is to alert us to the forfeiture of enormous future financial wealth that is the likely consequence of the way we often spend—unconsciously mis-allocating our dollars. In pointing out this forfeiture, the book also shows the magnitude of potential, future financial wealth that will result from a revised allocation of our spending dollars.

Spending is as easy as riding a bike.

Chapter 2

The Problem with Normal

"We have met the enemy, and he is us."
— Walt Kelly's Pogo

When it comes to spending and investment, we will see that we're all normal, that we make normal mistakes, usually without thinking, and that we can change our unconscious spending behavior to achieve actual wealth. But before we can do this, we need to understand what normal means.

Normal is not the same as average—the statistician's way to lop off all the interesting differences that make us human. Normal means much more. In the world of flesh-and-blood human beings, no one is average, but most of us are normal. In a nutshell, the basic thoughts and actions that are common to our species—despite our infinite differences—are what make us normal. It does not protect us from folly, but most of us are there.

A key aspect of being normal is the fact that we do things for valid, predictable reasons. The principal one of these is to survive. Our innate desire to continue living, preferably without discomfort or trauma, drives us to find ways to meet our needs. Mere survival is not all. We also want to thrive and to satisfy our many needs and wants. This makes things complicated.

Being Normal Doesn't Mean Being Right

Frank Capra's classic film, *It's A Wonderful Life*, is a celebration of ordinary, quirky people leading outwardly ordinary lives. The setting is commonplace—apart from a visiting angel and an alternate version of history, of course. The characters are remarkably normal. We identify with them. They live and behave in normal ways, as most of us do.

But the movie's famous bank run scene shows how problematic normal can be. Ordinary people, sparked by news of the market crash and frightened by sirens and general chaos, descend on the Building & Loan to demand their money. The movie's hero begs them to think about what's really happening. He persuades them—barely—to reconsider their first impulse, and disaster is averted. As in real life, the most common, instinctive reaction of people to a crisis can be both perfectly normal and dead wrong.

We've all been there. An ordinary, routine situation changes unexpectedly. We automatically do the first thing that pops into our minds and, without knowing exactly what happened, we find ourselves in a ditch—sometimes a literal one. It happens without warning: driving to the store, speaking at a staff meeting, going on vacation, or trying to fix the sink. (Helpful hint: Turn off the water first.) Things were going so smoothly, events turn unexpectedly wrong, and our first, gut reaction has a really good chance of making things worse.

During World War II, American GIs invented a saying for this: SNAFU (Situation Normal, All Fouled Up).

The Basics of Bias

To understand why this happens, we must acknowledge an important fact of life: Everyone is biased. They are a natural and normal part of who we are. Often, however, the word bias conjures negative emotions, as in the case of unjust racial or gender-related discrimination. However, bias, in the broadest sense is simply our preference or inclination for or against something. It can be conscious or unconscious, positive or negative, subtle or obvious.

A bias is an information-processing shortcut, an inference or assumption based on previous experience that allows us to make decisions, rightly or wrongly, in an overwhelming sea of information. A completely unbiased human would not be able to function. They would waste vast amounts of time and energy trying to experience, analyze, and develop a response to everything.

Biases come from a combination of factors. One is our ability to remember, which is limited, and the need to sort, discard, and simplify information. Of necessity, we discard specifics and form generalities. We reduce events to their key elements. We edit and reinforce memories after the fact. We are also drawn to details that confirm our existing beliefs.

Some Common Human Biases:

- Complexity Bias
- Confirmation Bias
- The Curse of Knowledge and Hindsight Bias
- Frequency Bias
- Illusionary Ability Bias
- Illusionary Superiority Bias
- Negativity Bias
- Optimism/Pessimism Bias
- Recency Bias
- The Sunk Cost Fallacy

Bias also arises when we fail to understand the deeper meaning of our environment. We tend to simplify and see stories and patterns even when looking at incomplete data. We also feel the need to act quickly. To get things done, we focus on what we've already invested our time and energy in. We also favor simple-looking options over complex or ambiguous ones.

The list of normal, human biases is long. As discussed later in this book, many of them unconsciously influence our decisions when it comes to spending and wealth. For example, the Complexity Bias describes our tendency to give undue credence to complex concepts. Faced with two different choices over, let's say, investment strategy, it is perfectly normal for us to prefer a complex approach over a simple one. It just feels right, even when it's not. As we will see in Chapter 8, elaborate strategies based on regular buying and selling of individual stocks consistently produce results that are inferior to a simple approach, such as contributing regular amounts to an S&P 500 index fund and/or a Target Date fund—as outlined in Appendix A.

One such bias is the unwarranted confidence of beginners, known as the "Dunning Kruger Effect." This explains why new drivers have more accidents—and pay higher insurance premiums. It also explains why first-time investors tend to do more poorly than experienced ones. Such investors feel that they understand the basics and are prone to making inaccurate assumptions and incorrect decisions.

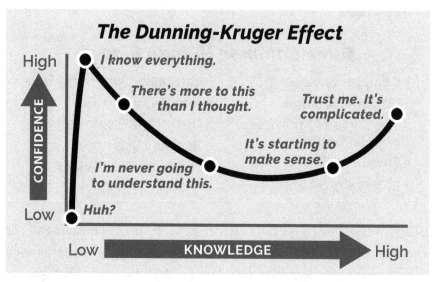

CAUTION: A small amount of knowledge may manifest itself in an unwarranted level of confidence, leading to inaccurate assumptions and incorrect answers.

Am I Biased?

The first step towards understanding these normal, human biases is to discover that we have them. We take unconscious mental short-cuts—because we are human—but we tend not to think of them as biases. Take some time to consider your own responses to everyday situations. For example, are there certain kinds of music or art that you either love or hate? That is a cultural bias. Do you prefer or dislike certain types of food, fashion, or entertainment? Do you have strong, "gut feelings" about pets, people of your own generation or another, or about your own family members? Each of these preferences or dislikes is something you experience with little conscious thought. In other words, it is a bias.

Some biases, particularly racial- or gender-related ones, are harmful and unjust. However, in many cases, a bias is neither right nor wrong. It's simply a personal preference put on autopilot. In any case, it is worth knowing that we have them. If a bias makes us prone to bad decisions, then it's time to reexamine and adjust them.

The problem is that our naturally occurring and completely normal human bias can lead us to a decision with harmful consequences. When a situation changes from our past experience, or if our bias was originally based on faulty or incomplete information, we follow our programming, so to speak, and experience poor results. Eventually, bad results may force us to confront a particular bias and change it, but humans can be a stubborn lot when it comes to change.

Financial bias (the subject of this book) is less obvious than those listed above. However, financial bias does follow the same pattern as the others and can lead to either good or bad results.

One thing is certain. Our preconceptions and mental shortcuts regarding spending and wealth are evidence that each of us is normal.

Reactive (System 1) and Reflective (System 2)

We meet our many needs and wants by making decisions and acting on them. Some of these decisions are unconscious and intuitive in nature, seemingly made automatically and without effort. Others are more deliberate and reasoned—the result of a conscious thought process. In his book, *Thinking, Fast and Slow*, psychologist and Nobel laureate Daniel Kahneman refers to these two modes of thinking by the labels System 1 and System 2 widely used by many psychologists.

In this book, we will also refer to them as Reactive or Reflective responses to a situation—like a scary dip in a stock market average.

Both of these modes are valid, very human responses. Intrinsically, they are neither right nor wrong. They are simply the ways we cope with incoming stimulus. When we first see the face of someone weeping, our negative, Reactive interpretation is largely automatic and subliminal (System 1). She is sad, we suppose. Then, after learning the context, our Reflective (System 2) abilities realize that the person was celebrating a one-point win in a basketball game. Our initial reaction was perfectly normal, but wrong.

When we see a written math problem, we recognize it as such, but most of us are unlikely to unconsciously or intuitively (System 1) come up with the answer. If we try, we are likely to get it wrong, as was the case with the ball-and-bat question in Chapter 1. To get the right answer, most of us would engage more deliberately (System 2) and work out the problem with paper and pencil.

Because we'll be referencing Kahneman's thesis throughout this book, it may be helpful to quote his definitions. You are encouraged to bookmark this page or highlight the definitions.

> " **System 1** operates automatically and quickly, with little or no effort and no sense of voluntary control."
>
> " **System 2** allocates attention to the effortful mental activities that demand it, including complex calculations."

The Reactive mode of thinking is an engrained part of our species' history of survival. Eons ago, reacting instantly to the presence of a large predator was literally a life-saving response. It became a characteristic that our uneaten ancestors passed down to us.

Our ability to do this serves us well today. Our Reactive, System 1 brains let us put routine matters on auto-pilot, so to speak, and conserve our limited Reflective, System 2 responses. No longer a pure survival mechanism, our habit patterns help us cope with our ever more complicated lives.

Just for fun, think of the things you do every day without a lot of conscious thought. They range from the mundane, like using a knife and fork or tying your shoes, to the more specialized, like using a computer or mobile device at work. When you first learned to do them, it required a lot of conscious, Reflective energy. After they became routine, it required much less.

Driving to the Store

As an experiment, try to recall the specific actions you took the last time your drove to a grocery store. Unless something extraordinary happened on the way, there will be many blanks. You arrived at your destination with little memory of what turns you made, how you maintained a safe distance from other cars, whether you obeyed traffic rules, or even what you saw or heard on the way.

Routine driving is an example of Reactive behavior. It is cognitively easy. It requires only nominal conscious effort. You mind is free for other things, like listening to music or conversing casually with a fellow passenger.

The routine act of driving is behaviorally automatic. But if something out of the ordinary happens on the road ahead, then your conscious, Reflective brain re-engages to deal with the new situation. Conversations and other actions unrelated to driving cease.

This wasn't the case when you learned how to drive. Your conscious, Reflective process was fully active as you learned to steer, use the pedals, enter traffic, and parallel park. In fact, you were probably too conscious during the learning process, making mistakes like over-steering or braking too suddenly. But gradually, and with plenty of practice (and an instructor or companion with patience and courage), you developed the intuitive habits that embody being a good driver. You transferred a set of learned, Reflective behaviors to a set of semi-automatic, Reactive behaviors.

The System Shift and the Lazy Controller

Let's start by recognizing that we all tend to be lazy at times. It's part of our evolutionary heritage—to assure that we have sufficient energy to run from dangerous situations, like the approach of a man-eating beast. It's not a pejorative or degrading term, it's merely a statement of fact. It also helps explain why we delegate many actions to our Reactive brains. So long as these activities remain routine and predictable, they require little expenditure of energy and we do them without much thinking, and usually do them well. But as soon as there is a change in the environment, our once-automatic activity changes.

Try another experiment. While walking and chatting casually with a friend, bring up a serious topic and observe what happens. Invariably, she or he will slow down. (If you're really friends, you'll slow down too.) Kahneman posed a similar experiment. He asked a walking companion to compute 23 times 78 in his head. The friend stopped in his tracks. He shifted away from a routine Reactive activity to focus on a more demanding process.

Like physical exertion, conscious, Reflective activity requires effort. Because our normal tendency is to conserve finite mental and emotional resources, we are prone to take the path of least resistance. Letting our unconscious, Reactive brain take over—responding intuitively and impulsively—is all too common, especially when we are stressed or tired or mentally exhausted. We have what Kahneman refers to as a Lazy Controller. That's not an insult, just a natural, self-protective part of being human. We focus on what we perceive as the single, most important thing. Out of necessity, we delegate seemingly less immediate or important tasks to our Reactive, System 1 nature.

The Hazards of Being Normal

Acting intuitively and spontaneously is not a bad thing. It can be remarkably successful. A well-trained athlete, artist, or mathematician spends less energy performing complex tasks in his or her area of expertise than they did while learning to do it. It appears effortless and natural. But some have suggested that intuition alone—the ability to think without thinking—is an intrinsically superior mode of thinking. It is not.

Of course, part of us wants to believe that intuition is superior. Things that are more familiar or easier to figure out seem truer than things that are novel, difficult to see, or require hard thought. (As we'll see, that's an example of a type of thinking error called "cognitive ease." See Appendix E.)

The problem is, our intuition may not be founded in fact or in deliberately cultivated habits, but in presuppositions, cognitive illusions, and biases. Our response may seem natural, even easy, but it can be wrong, and lead to bad or at least ineffective results. It results in a situation that is totally normal, but all fouled up.

The most common way our intuitive, Reactive habits lead us astray is when an environment is different from the one to which we are accustomed. What was "normal-smart" in one situation can become "normal-stupid" in another. As we will see, when allowed to occur in the realm of spending, "normal-stupid" can have disastrous financial consequences.

Looking Both Ways

In North America and most European and Asian countries, vehicles travel on the right side of the road. As a result, pedestrians crossing the road habitually look left first, before looking right and then left again. Most of us do this without thinking—for good reason: the potential hazard from oncoming traffic is more immediate to a pedestrian's left, because cars use the right side.

But in the United Kingdom and Australia, the opposite is true. Vehicles use the left side of the road, and pedestrians look right first before crossing. Two different groups of people have developed Reactive coping habits which are literally 180 degrees apart.

An American who travels to London has exactly the wrong instinct when about to cross a busy street. The likelihood of unintended mayhem was not good for tourism. So, at many London pedestrian crossings, you will see—in large letters—the words "LOOK RIGHT." It's an attempt to adjust an unconscious but potentially fatal habit.

Changing habits to cope with new situations is difficult but not impossible. When Sweden switched from left-side to right-side driving in 1967, temporary chaos ensued—despite months of planning and public announcements. Change is possible, however-er. With practice and

Switching from driving on one side of the road to another can be chaotic. (Stockholm on September 3, 1967. Photo by JanCollsiöö - Så var det, Public Domain)

patience, people can unlearn a potentially harmful response and learn a different one. In Sweden today, a pedestrian's instincts are the same as those in America—but both must use caution when in the U.K. or Australia.

There are also ingrained habits for which the negative consequences are vague or unknown—giving you no reason to change them. Think about some things you do automatically that have no actual results. Have you ever done any of the following:

Checked your email within five minutes of checking it the last time?

Pressed the button repeatedly when summoning an elevator?

Pushed on a door when the sign reads "pull"?

An automatic response can be both perfectly normal and wrong at the same time. Our Reactive habits also make us bad guessers. As proof, if you haven't done so already, answer the five questions at the beginning of Chapter 1.

Making Things Worse

Our tendency to do things Reactively is more pronounced, and more likely to have unfortunate consequences, when we feel a sense of urgency. As our lives becomes more hectic and complex, we have less time to pause and consider things Reflectively. According to the Association for Psychological Science, when people under stress are making a difficult decision, they tend to pay more attention to the potential upside and less to the downside. They also find it more difficult to control their urges. Getting immediate relief becomes more important than the potentially negative consequences.

Decisions made in response to urgent, immediate stimulus carry a greater risk when it comes to spending and investing. (In Chapter 8, we will discuss how all the "noise" can increase our sense of perceived urgency, preventing us from making conscious, Reflective decisions.)

While there is no panacea for making our lives simpler, it is important to recognize that part of being normal is making decisions under less-than-ideal circumstances. To help activate your Reflective nature, begin by asking, "Is this really urgent or does it only feel urgent?"

Resistance to Change

Changing our Reactive behavior is no small task. As natural conservers of our own energy, we resist change as a matter of course. If the positive incentive for changing our behavior is too small—or unknown—then we ignore the results and continue doing the same thing. If the negative consequences are remote or seemingly insignificant, then the same thing happens—nothing. But sometimes, our resistance to change entails unnecessary risk.

Fasten Your Seatbelts!

First developed for automobiles in the 1950s, seatbelts have a scientifically proven benefit: Your chance of death or injury is far lower if you wear them. Convincing motorists to use them is another matter. Since their introduction, and despite increasingly strict "click-it or ticket" laws, some motorists resist, especially when the trip is "only a few blocks to the store."

The problem? Our normal, Reactive brains see the present (where accidents are statistically rare) as *more real* than the consequences of an accident that has not yet happened. We unconsciously discount risk and resist an inconvenient change in behavior.

Automakers' earlier, psychological solutions had mixed results. If seatbelts were not used, an annoying beep or tone sounded immediately and continuously. It did not stop until the seatbelts were fastened. However, users would sometimes fasten the seatbelts permanently and sit on them—or disable the warning system altogether.

As a better solution, carmakers created a seatbelt warning that emitted intermittent audio sounds. The first chimes or tones were a gentle reminder, followed by a pause, and then a series of increasingly loud and strident beeps. The annoyance factor grew, not so rapidly that the user was motivated to disable the warning system. It was just annoying enough to make wearing seatbelts the lesser of two evils. Over time, the act of fastening one's seatbelt becomes automatic.

Seatbelt use is not yet universal, of course. But with a combination of strict laws and more subtle warning systems, it is becoming more common. The acknowledged benefit (living) is supported by a Reactive, System 1 habit.

Let's go back to an example cited earlier: checking your email (or Twitter feed or Facebook posts) every few minutes. There is increasing evidence that doing so out of habit is extremely costly—sapping our productivity. According to a 2008 University of California Irvine study , "The cost of interrupted work: more speed and stress," it can take an average of over 23 minutes to return one's focused attention to a task after being interrupted. The more engaging the interruption, the harder it is to switch back.

However, merely knowing about that long-term cost does not automatically equip us to cease our Reactive habits. We are resistant to change when given the choice of easy versus difficult. It's perfectly normal to drop everything and look, even when we know the email will be mostly spam and the posts filled with distracting nonsense. The act of checking creates an emotional reward—seemingly meeting the need for connection. The negative consequences are less clear, and the Reflective effort (not looking) more daunting.

The Roundabout Riddle

More common in Europe, well-designed traffic circles or roundabouts are slowly gaining acceptance in North America. They are demonstrably more efficient, compared with traffic-lighted or four-way stop intersections.

However, public resistance to roundabouts is a good example of normal, unconscious, Reactive bias.

When roundabouts are first proposed in a community, the most common objection is that people aren't used to them, which they believe will result in more accidents. They don't feel the same as a four-way stop, so we resist the idea of learning new habits.

What overcomes our unconscious bias is experience. We learn subtle visual cues, like the direction of the other car's front tires. Gradually, our habits change, and our confidence grows.

Just for fun, consider your own biases on the subject of roundabouts. If such intersections are rare or nonexistent where you live, what is your first, gut reaction to them? If they already have been implemented, what's your attitude?

Practice and Patience

Despite our innate resistance to change, it is entirely possible to adjust our habit behavior from "normal-stupid" to "normal-smart." In his excellent book, *The Power of Habit*, Charles Duhigg notes that "changes are accomplished because people examine the cues, cravings, and rewards that drive their behaviors and then find ways to replace their self-destructive routines with healthier alternatives." Such change is more likely when we believe change is possible—something that is more likely in a group context than when we go it alone.

So, in the case of constantly checking email or social media, knowing the reward of doing so less often (being more productive) is only one step. The other is recognizing the craving (the need to connect) and substituting a different activity, such as regularly connecting with actual humans, in order to meet the need.

The roundabout illustration given earlier is an imperfect example of changing our Reactive, System 1 biases, because the change—to a more efficient system—is not an individual choice but a government-mandated one. However, it is a good illustration of how our biases can in fact have less than ideal results. What seems intuitively right is actually preventing long-term success, both in getting to your literal destination (traffic) and your financial one (spending). Our natural response to financial stimulus, like the craving for a new car or the gut reaction to a short-term stock drop, will often put us in a metaphorical traffic jam. A familiar-seeming situation is not what it appears to be, so your instincts result in poor outcomes.

Change is possible, however. The first step is to recognize that our Reactive habits are completely normal—a part of our energy-conserving nature, if not our literal survival. They are also prone to numerous biases and thinking errors. The next step is to know the full extent of what our automatic, Reactive response actually costs, not only in the distant future but also in the present. We also need to be constantly reminded—as with the intermittent seatbelt warning—that a different action is possible. Perhaps the most important factor is our belief that a different behavior, reinforced by a group of positive, change-minded peers, will satisfy the basic need in a far more satisfying manner. With practice and patience—and the support of others—we will discover that once-unfamiliar habits can help us reach our goal.

Asking Questions

In Chapter 10, we have posed a series of questions related to each chapter. For the moment, however, let's consider just one:

What normal action has recently led me to a result that was different from the one I expected?

The answer does not have to relate to spending. It can be as simple as pushing on a door when the sign reads "pull." The point is to remember something that was perfectly normal and also wrong.

Tania's "light-bulb moment."

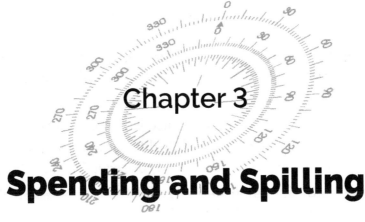

Chapter 3

Spending and Spilling

*"I love money. I love everything about it. I bought some pretty
good stuff. Got me a $300 pair of socks. Got a fur sink. An
electric dog polisher. A gasoline powered turtleneck sweater. And,
of course, I bought some dumb stuff, too."*
— Steve Martin

Once we recognize how normal we really are—thinking both fast and
slow, as Kahneman describes it—it's easier to figure out how and why
we spend our money, our time, and our resources. Spending is not an
impersonal transaction. It's a personal choice governed by our emotions as well as our rational thoughts.

As with most human activity, spending is complicated. For good or ill,
it is affected by our personal, subjective biases. Consciously or unconsciously, we continuously spend in ways that produce wealth—or in
ways that have the opposite effect.

Spending and Spilling

Spending is a choice, a decision to give something of value in exchange for something else of value. It involves more than just money.
Spending also involves time, energy, and effort—the things for which
money is a convenient proxy. It also includes intangible but very real
things such as reputation and trust.

We spend in order to meet a need or satisfy a want or desire. Very
often, however, we fail to consciously and deliberately weigh the full
value—including the future value—of the thing received in exchange.
We trust our normal, intuitive feelings about the exchange. As a result,

we can spend more than the actual need requires—often many times more than we realize. This is a phenomenon we call spilling.

Spilling can result from an entire transaction or just part of one. It is the amount spent in excess of what could have been spent on a perfectly suitable, lower-cost alternative. It is difficult to detect precisely because of our normal, *Reactive* (System 1) behavior. We are primed, by our advertising-driven culture, among other things, to make spending decisions more or less automatically. It is cognitively easier to take mental shortcuts, spilling money, rather than use our *Reflective* (System 2) abilities to consider the long-term outcome.

As we will discover, spilling is something we do almost every day, whether we're aware of it or not. To understand the idea better, let's look at a common situation:

An Illuminating Example

Consider Tania Gilman, a successful, 20-something professional with a growing family and a busy but rewarding urban lifestyle. She began her promising tech career by graduating at the top of her class and landing a job in a leading software firm. Like many of her peers, she often works at odd hours from her home office. Tania works and relaxes in a well-lit, indoor environment. Moving frequently to different parts of her home, the idea of turning out lights in unused rooms does not often occur to her. When it does, in the form of her father's well-remembered quip, "So, you work for the electric company now?" she sighs, but nothing more. It's a small thing in the midst of such a full and busy life.

In a way, she's not wrong. The cost of a regular light bulb, left on for 12 hours, comes to about 14 cents a day. Let's assume that the total number of bulbs—controlled by three or four wall switches in various places—illuminating empty rooms for 12 hours is an even dozen. Adding up all the resulting kilowatts spent, the total is an unremarkable sum of $1.68 per day. You can probably guess where this is going. Assuming this spending continues from age 27 until Tania and her husband reach retirement age at 67, they will have irrevocably spent the remarkable sum, adjusted for probable inflation, of a little over $77,680

If that was the only moral of the story, it would be interesting but not alarming. Considering that Tania and her husband will earn and spend far more than that in their lifetimes, this kind of spending seems reasonable. But the story has a twist, because the amount spilled is far more than $77,680. If that same amount was spent differently—let's say, in a no-commission, index fund with an average, long-term growth rate of 10%—the resulting value (also adjusted for inflation) *would likely be over $367,895!*

Why would an industrious, intelligent person forfeit over a quarter million dollars by spending, or rather spilling, a comparatively small sum of money? Tania is not a spendthrift or a fool. The problem is that she's a normal human being.

As we saw in Chapter 2, her conscious, Reflective reasoning process—what Kahneman defines as System 2 behavior—is used to make important, often complicated decisions. Of necessity, other decisions are managed by her unconscious habits—her Reactive, System 1 behavior. Flipping light switches falls into this category. It is one example of a large class of decisions that are the subject of this book: how normal people spend money, and the effect of that spending on financial wealth.

A REALLY IMPORTANT NOTE:

Throughout this book, we will often talk about the negative, unseen implications of spending small amounts of money. This does not mean that merely curtailing such spending will automatically result in great wealth. One must take the next step: purposefully investing in something that will likely grow in value over time. The mechanics for doing this are spelled out in Chapter 9 and in Appendix A.

Also, keep in mind that these small amounts, such as Tania's $1.68, are not the amounts you would be depositing on a daily basis in a low-cost index fund. Rather, as outlined in Appendix A, these small spending amounts, from multiple sources, should be combined into a monthly total and used to determine how much to regularly allocate to an index fund.

Finally, the term "index fund" itself may be unfamiliar. In Chapter 8, we describe this concept in detail. For now, however, we'll rely on Investopedia, which defines an index fund as "a type of mutual fund with a portfolio constructed to match or track the components of a financial market index, such as the Standard & Poor's 500 Index (S&P 500)." Many investment firms offer S&P 500 index funds, some at lower costs than others. This lets you invest in many companies at once, namely the 500 largest U.S. companies, rather than picking individual stocks.

Spending as a National Pastime

Spending is part of the background noise we take for granted. The average American, we are told, will spend between $2.5 and $4.5 million in their lifetime. The Consumer Spending Index and the Gross Domestic Product (GDP)—the total value of goods and services provided in a year's time—are taken as gospel for how well or how poorly the economy is doing. But as individuals, we seldom think about the nature of spending itself.

Spending—the exchange of one thing of value for another—falls into two categories. First, it can be for *things that will likely decline in financial value over time*. These range from immediate consumables, such as electricity, to durable goods that eventually wear out or otherwise depreciate. It is also for experiences such as movies or vacations. While the memories may last a lifetime, they are not convertible into anything that can be spent again. All such spending, from lighting to laptops to luxury vacations, is irreversible.

The other spending category is for *things that have a potential to increase in value over time.* This includes some physical objects, such as art or other collectibles, but more often includes real estate, stocks and bonds, and bank accounts. It also includes certain intangibles such as education and training, so long as the acquired knowledge or skills are a source of future financial wealth in the form of higher earnings.

The Nature of Wealth

The measure of economic and personal success or failure—wealth—will be discussed in Chapter 6. Like spending, wealth is an idea we seldom examine in detail. Instead, we tend to view it from our unconscious biases. Many believe that wealth is desirable, but few consciously think about what it is or why we are driven to pursue it.

Wealth is complicated. It has a financial element, of course, but it also has emotional and aspirational components. Wealth represents *an ability to meet a need or a want—and an assurance of being able to do so in the future.* The need can be purely *utilitarian*—something that ensures our physical existence. It can also be *emotional*—something that enhances our sense of well-being and fulfillment. Of course, the need can also be *expressive*—the desire to create or reinforce one's self-image or sense of purpose.

Not only do we gloss over the meanings of spending and wealth, we also connect the two in ways that limit our success. For example, we assume that wealth and spending always occur in a certain order. We believe we must first obtain wealth—preferably lots of it—before we can spend as much as we desire. However, this one-way view holds true only for spending on things that are likely to *decline* in value. What we miss is the connection going the other way—spending for things that are likely to *increase* in value. As we will see, some kinds of spending actually produce wealth.

But that leaves us with the same question we asked about Tania's lighting decision or, rather, her unwillingness to make a different decision: *Why do we ignore or disregard spending habits that have such an impact on our long-term wealth potential?* Even when we know about the different kinds of spending, the complex nature of wealth, and how the two are connected, *what prevents us from making spending decisions that will create greater wealth?*

Decision-Making Biases

In Chapter 2, we discussed a concept at the heart of this book: the personal biases that govern our decision-making without our conscious reasoning. Kahneman likens these computations in our brains to dials in an airplane cockpit, each dial indicating the current value of an essential variable. Readouts of these variables occur systematically and automatically. Only when a dial indicates a problem does the brain switch from the unconscious, Reactive mode to the extra effort required by Reflective reasoning.

An important concept in this metaphor is *cognitive ease*—the combination of repeated experience, mood, and other unconscious factors that make a particular action feel familiar, effortless, and generally positive. When we experience cognitive ease, we feel comfortable but are likely to be superficial in our thinking. When the opposite occurs—*cognitive strain*—we become more vigilant and less error-prone, sometimes at a cost to our creativity, but we do so under protest because, as normal human beings, we prefer ease over strain. Tania's lighting routine involves a high level of cognitive ease. So, she is disinclined to welcome her dad's voice in her head or spend effort thinking about the long-term consequences of spending (or, rather, not investing) a mere $1.68 per day.

Related to cognitive ease is another Reactive decision-making bias called *priming*—the conscious or subconscious exposure to an idea that inclines us to think about an associated idea. There are few areas more impacted by priming than our spending and wealth.

Consumer advertising involves a great deal of emotional priming, fueled by targeted data algorithms. Increasingly, personalized ads are overwhelmingly geared towards spending on things likely to decline in value. Gratification of *immediate* needs—even those that appear lofty or aspirational—is prioritized. We are primed to make spending choices that offer expressive and emotional benefits over mere utilitarian ones. This is expected and even necessary in a competitive consumer marketplace, but it contributes to a level of cognitive ease that makes it harder for us to spend effort on critical, Reflective thinking.

One great misperception about spending money stems from the ease with which we can acquire additional spendable money. Specifically, this includes spending credit card-borrowed money on things which are normally declining-value items. Such spending adds the expense of credit card interest repayment to the original spending on non-appreciating items. This further reduces the amount of money that can be spent on appreciating assets (investments).

Attitude and Behavior: Investorship

Sheer willpower is not the solution to the spilling problem, especially when the spilling is largely unconscious. Tania's father's adage about not leaving lights on may have created a sense of guilt but did not provide a reliable way to consistently shift from automatic, Reactive thinking into a more Reflective mindset.

The answer lies in an approach to spending that we call Investorship. As we will explore in later chapters, this idea holds that an individual's *attitude and behavior* relative to spending, investing, and investments play a major role in determining the investment outcome. The best way to reveal those attitudes and reinforce different behavior when it comes to spending is to ask questions. When confronted with a spending decision, always ask the following:

> **1 – Stop! Have I thought this through? Is this spending urgent or does it only SEEM urgent?**
>
> **2 – What are the present needs being met by this particular spending decision?**
>
> **3 – What are the future needs that will be met (or NOT met) by this spending?**
>
> **4 – What are ALL my spending choices in this case?**

Consider the importance of the first Investorship question: "Have I thought this through?" Too often, when making a routine spending decision, we allow an easy presupposition to substitute for a full analysis of the actual numbers. Tania and her husband feel that lighting is "just a hassle" or "not worth the bother," rather than considering the long-term spilling of their future wealth. When it comes to challenging our normal, cognitive illusions, "thinking it through" is a useful habit—for seemingly small investments as well as large purchases.

Question 4 poses an interesting exercise when it comes to Tania's spilling problem. If the problematic spending on lighting unused rooms could be eliminated *entirely*, then so could the spilling of nearly a quarter million dollars. That solution is unlikely, however. It is difficult to automate turning off lights in unused rooms. It's also problematic to do so manually on a consistent basis. But what if there was a reasonable spending *alternative*—say, LED light bulbs—that reduced both the immediate spending and therefore the long-term spilling?

In Appendix B, you'll find more detailed examples of spending and spilling consequences (or you can discover your own, using the online Investorship Calculator, Appendix B.) Suffice it to say that if enough of these spending changes were made—from things that decline in value to those that potentially increase in value—then significant wealth will be the predictable result.

Deal or No Deal?

Buying a car is another example of spending that can easily become spilling. An acquaintance of ours, Kevin Hodges, age 40, is a reasonably well-informed consumer. He regularly avails himself of public information about car performance and safety ratings. He is aware of automakers' skill at marketing the image of their products—priming their audience with non-stop advertising—and of car salespeople's skills in "reading" a prospective buyer. Unfortunately, his store of useful knowledge did not include Investorship basics.

Last year, Kevin bought a new model car for $10,000 more than the cost of a used model, three years older, in excellent condition, and with nearly identical features. Focused on the immediate situation, he unconsciously spilled a great deal of future wealth.

As with the light bulb example, the spilling is not immediately obvious. The one-time spending difference of $10,000 is not a remarkable sum for Kevin, who can afford a high-end vehicle. Both cars will be of negligible resale value in 40 years. Service costs will be only marginally higher for the used car over the same time period. The real issue is the difference in future value over time. If that same $10,000 was spent differently—say, in a low-cost index fund with an average, long-term growth rate of 10%—the resulting value after 40 years (adjusted for inflation) *would likely be over $452,592!*

Like Tania, Kevin is no fool. His spending is based on meeting a complex array of needs—transportation, efficiency, safety, self-expression, and status. These needs are perfectly normal. Many are even subconscious. But in the midst of making that complex spending decision, however, Kevin failed to slow down and let his Reflective, System 2 process take full stock of the situation.

Needs and Wants

The reason to spend time, energy, or money is to satisfy a need or a want. So, an important aspect of Investorship is to examine the need or want we are satisfying—and our motivation for doing so. Is it beneficial, and to whom? Is it reasonable in light of other needs and wants? Perhaps the most significant question is about time. Is the *present* need important enough to risk forfeiting the ability to meet a *future* one?

Self-Transcendence Needs
Need to find meaning and
identity beyond the self

Self-Actualization Needs
Need to live up to our
fullest and unique potential

Esteem Needs
Need for self-esteem, achievement,
competence, and independence; need for
recognition and respect from others

Belongingness & Love Needs
Need to love and be loved, to belong
and be accepted; need to avoid
loneliness and separation

Safety Needs
Need to feel that the world is organized and
predictable; need to feel safe, secure, and stable

Physiological Needs
Need to satisfy hunger and thirst

Maslow's Hierarchy of Needs (Illustration courtesy of David Myers)

In 1943, psychologist Abraham Maslow theorized the now popular "hierarchy of needs" to explain human motivation. Usually represented as a pyramid, the theory holds that needs at one level must be satisfied before motivation to meet needs at the next level can occur. For example, physiological needs such as hunger and thirst must be largely met before the needs of safety, security, and stability.

Maslow's original theory held that lower-level needs must be *completely* satisfied before moving on to a higher pursuit. However, modern theory holds that these levels of need overlap one another and that lower levels may take precedence over others at any point in time.

When it comes to spending, there is another factor to consider. If we have erroneous, inflated notions of our belonging or self-esteem needs—especially those in the immediate present—then we are prone to taking shortcuts. These can be hazardous to our ability to meet future needs. For example, to attain a perceived, immediate "higher need," for status or esteem, we may satisfy our physiological needs with cheap, unhealthy food. The resulting health problems will in turn endanger our ability to meet future needs. We may also attempt to satisfy legitimate, higher needs (as Kevin did) without sufficient regard for long-term consequences.

The needs at the higher end of Maslow's spectrum are valid, even if they are more difficult to quantify and assign a spending value. *The problem occurs when we confuse needs and wants.* The latter (wants) is a craving for satisfaction—as defined by others—that often fails to materialize even when the desired object is obtained.

The motivations driving Kevin's decision were mostly about the *present*. He intuitively believed that his needs for transportation, efficiency, safety, self-expression, and status would be met by a new car over a used one. What he failed to do is consider the impact of his spilling on his *future* ability to meet those same needs.

The higher we go in the hierarchy of needs, the more likely we are to confuse needs and wants. There we are also more likely to commit thinking errors and presuppositions—cognitive illusions based in our normal, Reactive thinking.

For example, we may believe, like Kevin, that a new car confers more status and elicits more respect than a used one. The more we believe that to be true, the easier it is to jump to the conclusion that $10,000 extra is well worth it. (This is known in social psychology as *confirmation bias*—the predisposition to find reasons for a decision that confirms what we already believe.) We've replaced a legitimate need with a want—a craving that is more easily manipulated and more likely to result in spilling.

Other thinking errors make us prone to mistaking wants for needs, leading to poor spending decisions. Our normal, Reactive brain tends to fill in gaps caused by incomplete data by substituting unwarranted confidence in our assumptions. We're inclined to believe a well-presented sales pitch and gloss over the possibility of missing data. We are also strongly influenced by first impressions—including those made by really skilled car salespeople—making us less likely to pause, analyze, and exercise our Reflective powers.

This problem is not limited to big-ticket items or to higher-level needs. Consumer product advertising is notorious for creating demand for branded products (bottled water, name-brand clothing, and prepared foods, to name a few). Here too, the basic, physical need of Maslow's model has been conflated with a want. We allow our biased, Reflective brain to uncritically spend, based on a familiar, cognitively easy-to-grasp story—which is the whole point of effective marketing. When that causes us to spill, we forfeit the ability to better meet our needs in the future.

Saving IS Spending

So far, we have discussed spending and spilling in terms of services (lighting) or durable goods (cars)—things that do not retain value. But when it comes to things that increase in value, we also make the same kind of spending errors.

One of the great misconceptions about spending is that we have only two, mutually-exclusive options for what we do with our money: spend it or save it. This tends to suggest that spending and saving are polar opposites. Since people view saving as something they do with money that isn't spent, and since most people spend everything, they find themselves with no money left to save.

If you identify with this view, you're not alone. Many people feel they cannot save, much less invest. Or if they invest nominally, in a 401(k) plan or otherwise, it feels woefully inadequate. Bills rise inevitably to meet income, and then some. So long as we view spending and saving as mutually exclusive, the problem seems insurmountable.

However, spending and saving are not opposites. The truth is that, while we're alive, unless we hoard or give our money away, *we spend everything*. Activities thought of as saving, such as annuities or regular savings accounts, result in an admittedly small something in exchange. So, by definition, saving is spending, even if the financial return is small and the emotional satisfaction is different from other forms of spending.

Spilling for a Rainy Day

Janelle Powers was taught from an early age to save money and defer immediate gratification in order to spend money later on something she really wanted. This habit serves her well. At age 32, her well-paying job enables her to put about $150 per week into a savings account, from which she can make occasional withdrawals to meet unexpected expenses.

What Janelle does not consciously realize is that her benign habit of saving is actually a choice to spend on a savings account. Let's assume that her withdrawals from the savings account are modest, and that her average weekly contributions to the account—from age 32 through retirement at age 67—are closer to $120. At a typical interest rate of 3%, that would mean her bank spending will result in an approximate bank balance of about $596,648—assuming that she makes no withdrawals. Not bad, except for the fact that Janelle has spilled far more of her potential wealth.

With the same contribution amount over the same period, but in a low-cost index fund with an average, long-term growth rate of 10%—the resulting value after 35 years (adjusted for inflation) *would likely be over $2,254,295!* Like Tania and Kevin, she has made a spending choice from common, normal biases and habits rather than from an Investorship approach to spending and wealth.

Considering the Future and the Past

It is essential that all spending be given the benefit of Reflective thinking. It needn't take long—perhaps just a moment to recognize that the spending allocation has a sizable long-term consequence. Almost always, the decision can be delayed until there is sufficient time to think through the expenditure more fully.

However, our normal responses to spending and saving situations are often based on cognitive illusions and *instinct*. We *feel* that the meeting of an immediate need—however valid—can be done easily, by our Reactive habits, rather than by spending the energy to examine the facts closely. We are then more prone to wishful thinking, priming, and other biases. If these intuitive leaps happen to be correct, fine, but if not, we put our futures at risk.

Perhaps the most serious risk of spilling occurs because we do not fully consider our future needs. This is understandable, since we cannot know the future, and are experiencing only the present. Our needs occupy our attention, as they must. Rather than think about the complex uncertainty of the future, our brains prefer what Kahneman calls a *heuristic*—a mental shortcut that allows us to make decisions quickly and easily, but not always correctly. We tend to substitute an easier, simplified notion for the process of examining the facts in detail.

For Tania, the heuristic shortcut is, "I'm too busy to think about a few lights. What's the harm?" For Kevin, it is, "A new car is just better than a used one." For Janelle, it is, "I feel safer with money in the bank." In fact, none of these beliefs are absolutely true or a complete picture. They *feel* true, however, and our normal brains tend to choose them over the task of analysis and considering our future.

When we spend, we tend to neglect or oversimplify our future needs. But we also fail to consider the past clearly. In all three of our examples, the people have emotionally normal memories of past events—good or bad—that are anything but objective. Kevin's assumptions about cars may stem from pleasant memories and "that new car smell."

Janelle may simply be limited in her past experience with investments. Whatever the cause, it is perfectly normal to make assumptions and take the easier mental shortcut. But as we will find out, having a long view of past events and future probabilities is critical to Investorship spending. Ideally, each spending decision should be accompanied by the four Investorship questions discussed earlier.

When we choose to slow down and "think things through," several important things become clear:

- The past, although never a guarantee of what the future holds, always provides a basis for comparison, and a reasonable basis for approximating the future.
- Our needs in the future—from the physical to the aspirational—are almost always the same as those we have now. (We just can't imagine them as easily.)
- We spend everything (even when "saving"), but spending has different results on our ability to spend in the future.

As we turn from general spending to a very specific form of spending—financial investment—the principles for avoiding unnecessary spilling become even more important. Slowing down and thinking things through will help us avoid our natural biases and make decisions that will generate future wealth—both financial and otherwise.

Asking Questions

Before moving on to Chapter 4—on the particular form of spilling represented by credit cards—ask yourself the following question on the subject of spending in general:

What have I bought recently that has value now but will eventually have little or no value? (List as many things as you like.)

In Chapter 10, there are other questions about spending designed to help you pause, reflect, and engage your Reflective, System 2 faculties on this subject.

How Much Are You Spilling?

In the Epilogue and in Appendix A, you'll find a checklist for creating an investment account, setting up regular, automatic contributions to that account, and resisting the temptation to meddle with it—which affects its long-term value. But before you do this, it's helpful to know how much money you are actually spilling.

Starting now, use the form on the next page to write down your typical monthly purchases, what you paid, what you could have paid at a lower price (or by buying an acceptable substitute), and the difference. At the end of the month, add up those differences. If you're not into that much math, just add up the total amount spent each month and multiply it by a percentage—typically around 5 percent.

A Final Note

At www.investorship.com/content, you'll find a downloadable version of this form. Print out as many copies as you like to keep a regular monthly journal of your spilling. It will help you plan your wealth-building Investorship habits, as outlined in the Epilogue.

My Spilling Journal

Month: _____

Date	Purchase	Price	Better Price	Difference

Total spilled per month ⟶

— **OR** —

Total spilled per month ⟶ [____] x____% [____]

"I don't have any money, but I do have credit cards."

Chapter 4

Credit Cards and Spilling

"People who recognize that money won't buy happiness are still willing to see if credit cards will do the trick."
— E.C. McKenzie

Before moving on to a discussion of wealth, financial and otherwise, one particular form of spending must be addressed: the bank credit card. There is arguably no greater potential source of unnecessary spilling than the convenient plastic rectangle that occupies space in your wallet right now.

Credit itself can be beneficial in many ways. When a person or business lacks the immediate capital to make a purchase, credit from a bank can provide the needed funds for a fee in the form of interest. Credit based on the borrower's ability to repay is simply *future monetary capital* provided by a financial entity willing to take the risk.

Credit cards are an extension of the basic principle of credit, based on pre-approval of a certain amount of money. They give individuals the power to borrow and spend money today at will, always at the expense of future wealth. The card user is simply agreeing, with the bank's support, to defer payment to a later date.

Since their introduction in 1958, bank-issued credit cards have become the epitome of convenience, all but replacing cash and checks. While not immune to theft or fraud, credit cards also provide an array of electronic and institutional protections against unauthorized use. More recently, this has become even more convenient, as credit card accounts are added to our smartphones' digital wallets. Spending money with a credit card has never been easier.

When used responsibly, credit cards provide another benefit besides convenience. At the end of each month, a credit card statement is an accurate means of tracking one's expenses—whether for business or personal activity. Rather than store and sort a stack of paper receipts, users can rely on a single statement to manage and plan one's spending. At tax time, this can also reduce the hours needed to prepare a return. Both are legitimate reasons to use credit cards.

There is of course another reason for the growing use of credit cards. Our normal, human tendency is to avoid pain or at least reduce it in some way. If we can't reduce or eliminate pain, the next best option is to delay it. Spending money always involves an immediate sense of pain—specifically the pain of loss. However, using a credit card lets us delay that pain. The future where that pain will occur is sufficiently vague and far off to make the use of a credit card a much more attractive psychological choice. We therefore tend to choose what makes us feel better in the moment.

The Crux of the Problem

With credit cards, as with all other spending situations, we often let our *Reactive* (System 1) nature override our *Reflective* (System 2) reasoning. The latter requires more mental energy, so we quite naturally take the path that seems easier. In fact, the sheer convenience of using a credit card usually *feels* like the right decision in the short term.

The problem of course is that the long-term consequences of spending future wealth are seldom part of the decision. Most of us use credit cards with every intention of honoring our promise to repay—at *some* point in the future. The trouble is that credit card companies frequently make it easy not to pay back the entire amount, but to pay a minimum. A required minimum payment amount may be only two or three percent of the total, ostensibly easing your bill-paying burden. However, their seeming generosity has a downside we rarely consider.

The Minimum Payment Game

Let's start with a hypothetical purchase. You spot a new 60-inch, high-definition TV priced at only $1,000. It seems like a good deal, so you buy it and put it on your credit card. When your credit card statement arrives at the end of the month, you have the option of paying off the balance ($1,000) or paying it off at the minimum amount per month, typically two or three percent of the total borrowed. In making the decision of how much to pay, there are several things to consider.

On the Web, it is easy to find credit card calculators that will show how long it will take to pay off a credit card (and how much it will cost) if you only make minimum payments. Some calculators are even available on the websites of credit card companies themselves.

The results of using such a calculator are eye-opening. On the American Consumer Credit Counseling (ACCC) website, enter the following numbers for your hypothetical purchase:

Dollar Amount Charged.......... $1,000
Annual Interest Rate 18%
Minimum Payment Percent 2%
Minimum Payment Amount $20

The total interest charges in this TV example total $862.24, an additional 86% more money than the original amount, and would take *7.8 years* to pay off. But as frightening as this may be, too many people chose to make minimum payments rather than pay off the entire balance at the end of the month.

A far better alternative (besides not using the credit card in the first place) is to pay off the entire $1,000 when you get your credit card statement. Then, start putting $20 per month into a S&P 500 index fund. At the end of 7.8 years you fund will likely be worth over $3,000 (*three times the cost of the TV*).

The use of credit cards has a strong appeal to our normal, Reactive thinking. When we pay money for something, using a debit card, for example, the money is *gone*. At some level, we feel the pain of that loss, even if the purchase was warranted and met a legitimate need. Being able to seemingly avoid that pain is a normal desire, and because credit cards let us defer that pain in the moment, it becomes an easy decision. The fact that we have trouble visualizing the future pain makes it a difficult temptation to avoid.

However, by deferring the actual payment for our spending, we accomplish two undesirable outcomes. We spend our current financial wealth, very often on things that decrease in value. As we discussed in the previous chapter, this involves a great deal of unnecessary spilling. However, we also spend our *future* financial wealth, in the form of interest payments. Since we derive no actual value from the latter, it amounts to pure spilling.

Seeking Answers

According to a recent report on data released by the Federal Reserve, American credit card debt totaled over $935 billion. On average, they reported, Americans between the ages of 18 and 65 each had over $4,700 of credit card debt. Only 35% of credit card users actually paid off the balance at the end of the month, while most allowed balances to carry over. The report likened the phenomenon to addiction.

Of course, paying off a credit card completely each month is not an easy task. Doing so after letting balances accumulate is even harder. The solution is not simply a matter of willpower or luck, but an application of the Investorship principles presented in this book. By systematically choosing to exercise our Reflective capabilities, we can pause, consider the long-term consequences of spilling, and take steps to reallocate funds differently. Doing so will move us from simply being normal to becoming *normal plus*.

For example, many credit cards now offer cash back incentives—some more generous and unrestricted than others. Rather than consider such funds as spendable, a better course would be to make a regular, equivalent contribution to an index fund. However, the single most valuable decision is to *not* use credit cards to spend more that can be repaid at the end of the month. Being aware of the true spill potential of interest accrued by making minimum payments can be an ample reminder of the potential pain involved.

The same report describing the addictive nature of credit card debt also offered an interesting incentive to change one's behavior: the high return potential of paying down debt. According to the Fed, "Paying off credit card debt has a riskless return that averages 14 percent, which no other asset class can match."

Even for those who have allowed such balances to accumulate, the prospect of a high, risk-free return is attractive indeed.

Best Practices

A common mistake for those mired in credit card debt is to postpone other, positive actions until the debt is entirely cleared. This puts all the emphasis on deprivation and none on the prospect of increased wealth. As anyone trying to break a bad habit will confirm, this is a sure way to fail. Willpower alone (paying down the debt before investing anything) won't last.

Instead, no matter how large or small the debt may be, always take a two-fold approach. With that 14% riskless return in mind, pay down a healthy percentage of the outstanding debt. At the same time, allocate the same amount in a low-cost S&P 500 index fund, with "only" an average, long term return of 10%. Eventually, the card balance will be gone, and you can increase the regular allocation to building long-term wealth.

Using the Statement

No matter what your credit card balance may be, the monthly statement is a golden opportunity to engage in Investorship thinking.

First, it is usually wise to receive the statement on paper rather than electronically. Print is easier for viewing large amounts of information at once, while screen reading makes it more likely to miss details.

Every month spend approximately 20 minutes scanning the list of credit card charges. You will find two types of things:

Charges that are in some way illegitimate, including overcharges, possible fraud, and almost always a few "sneaky" charges. The latter occur when you sign up for a trial subscription or other promotional, free-for-30-days offer of some kind. Even when you intend to cancel, it's natural to forget a small charge.

Charges that beg the question, "did I need to spend that much?" This is subjective, of course, but a few moments' thought will often bring to mind ways that less money could have been spent—encouraging you to alter future behavior.

Be sure to note the amounts, however small, that your 20 minutes uncovers. If they add up to $50 a month on average, then you can make an interesting calculation:

$50 for 20 minutes work = $150/hour (not bad)

Of course, you can also make an even more important calculation. Suppose, starting at age 32, you made two such discoveries on your statements each month: each resulting in a similar charge reversal of $50 each. The monthly charge error total of $100, invested in a low-cost S&P 500 index fund with an average return of 10% *would potentially be worth approximately $433,518 in 35 years' time!*

The monthly credit card statement, far from being a tedious stack of paper, should be viewed as a welcome opportunity to plan your future wealth.

As with most of our Reactive-versus-Reflective thinking when it comes to spending, the use of credit cards is an exercise in deferred pain. All monetary spilling involves losing—usually at a much greater level than we imagined. Because we all hate to lose, there is hope that we can engage our reflective abilities more often, thinking more about the long-term consequences of our spending and less about the immediate gratification of a particular want.

Despite their perilous nature, credit cards provide an interesting view into our desire to spend. At worst, they allow us to defer the *actual* cost of spending and make the long-term consequences far worse than they should be. However, with sufficient application of Investorship thinking, credit card discipline can serve as a reminder to reallocate future wealth rather than spilling it.

"I got a great price: one-third off!"

Chapter 5

Understanding Price and Value

"Too many people today know the price of everything and the value of nothing."

— Ann Landers, paraphrasing Oscar Wilde

In previous chapters, we drew attention to the reality that all of us tend to spill far too much money unnecessarily, unconsciously every day, week, and year. This spilling often amounts to a loss of money resulting from our failure to differentiate between price and value.

If an item on a store shelf has its price reduced from $15 to $10 then we are quick to conclude that it may be a good value—but is it? Was its value ever $15 or was that a price placed on it so that the marked down price of $10 seemed like a good value. Questions like this are worthy of serious contemplation. By taking the time to understand and differentiate between price and value, enormous amounts of money spillage can be avoided.

Every day, online retail giant Amazon purportedly sells over 26 million items worldwide. Since Amazon's sales are said to constitute 5% of total retail sales, that means over 500 million items are being sold per day—or 6,000 per second. With so many transactions, each one requiring a mental consideration of value, worth, and price, it's no wonder we fail to properly differentiate these terms. Too often, we assume they are synonymous. Such a false conclusion is a *Reactive* (System 1) shortcut that replaces a more *Reflective* (System 2) process.

This explains many of the failures that occur in dealing with financial markets. Often, these failures result in tragic financial spilling.

In a nutshell, value is the usefulness or desirability of a product, service, or entity (home, business, etc.). Value has many attributes. It can be functional—offering some practical use over a known period of time. It can also be social—providing greater status or better connection with others. Of course, it can be psychological—providing personal satisfaction, fond memories, or other emotional benefits. Value is difficult to quantify, however, because individual humans and their circumstances are so varied. The value of a meal to someone who has just eaten is less than its value to someone who is hungry.

So, when someone perceives—subjectively—that something has value to him or her as a unique individual in a given situation, then that object or service has worth to that person. This perception varies from situation to situation, person to person, and even from moment to moment. However, the worth of a product or service to each individual will dictate what he or she is willing to give in exchange for it. Depending on the available supply (and the seller's perception of what it's worth to give it up), the resulting consensus has a dollar figure—the price.

Same Thing; Different Price

Consider a hypothetical situation. Shopper A is at a major chain supermarket intending to buy a quart of milk, while Shopper B is looking to do the same at a fashionable, upscale supermarket, famous for its cultural ambiance and its selection of healthy foods. Meanwhile, Shopper C has found a quart of milk at a local mini mart or convenience store. The price of each quart of milk—identical in every other aspect—is different. The difference is in the *perception* of each individual shopper.

The basic value of the product is roughly the same, no matter where it was bought. Milk satisfies a fundamental need for hydration. It also has nutritional, culinary, and aesthetic benefits.

However, because each shopper has different perceptions and circumstances, they each assign a different worth to the product at that moment. The chain store's broad selection of other products is worth something to Shopper A. The upscale supermarket's image of exclusivity and social status is worth something to Shopper B. The mini mart's primary advantage—convenience—is worth something to Shopper C. Each has embraced a premise and is willing to pay a different price for the exact same item.

How we *feel* about something we need or want—and about the circumstances surrounding it—influences our willingness to pay a price not directly connected to its value. It also turns out that we're not all that clear about value. Something can meet a genuine human need (*intrinsic* value) but be worth different things to different people (*economic* need). In some cases, it can even be worth nothing.

The Two Sides of Value

A good way to understand value is to take a deep breath of air. The air filling your lungs—or, to be more precise, the oxygen comprising 21% of it—has a high intrinsic value. It meets the most basic need in Maslow's hierarchy, although we seldom even think about it.

However, ordinary air with 21% oxygen has zero economic value—so long as it is not a scarce commodity. Air only becomes economically valuable when it is restricted, polluted, or degraded. When good, clean air becomes scarce, we are more likely to pay the costs of keeping clean air available. Additionally, since 100% pure oxygen (something not readily available in nature), may be required for medical or special applications, we assign an economic value to it and pay for it.

The Price & Value of a Refrigerator

The sale price of anything valuable—and relatively scarce—is a joint decision, agreed upon by the buyer and the seller. A significant number of buyers must believe that having a valuable product or service is worth spending a certain amount of money. The seller must also believe that that amount is fair. It must cover their costs plus a reasonable profit for taking the trouble to make it. To illustrate this, let's use an everyday example: a refrigerator.

Refrigerators have *intrinsic* value because they keep food from spoiling. This helps prevent illness, increase the variety of foods we consume, and reduce the frequency of trips to the store or to restaurants. However, their *economic* value is determined differently.

To the buyer of a refrigerator, its economic value is the *difference* between what he or she would be spending with it and without it. Most of us don't add up all the costs of not having a refrigerator, but we have a fairly good idea of its worth. On the other hand, to the seller of a refrigerator, its economic value is the *difference* between what he or she can buy and sell it—minus the costs involved. I may buy one refrigerator because of the greater cost of not having one. But I will only buy more than one if I can sell them profitably.

Needless to say, the actual price of a refrigerator varies widely, not only from model to model but also from day to day or from one part of the world to another. A newer model with improved features will command a different price than one that is older or worn out. Buyers in warmer climates will have a different idea of its economic value than those living in the arctic. When refrigerators with mechanical door locks were common—and the source of tragic deaths—models with child-safe locks commanded a higher price than they do now, when the feature is a government-mandated standard. A seller, anticipating the arrival of new models, will change the price of older ones to optimize inventory.

In other words, prices change rapidly, as conditions affect the buyers' and sellers' perception of current economic value. Even when an object's intrinsic value remains constant, and its overall economic value increases over time, its price in a given situation is an unreliable predictor of its actual value. This is true not only of refrigerators themselves but also of the companies that make them.

Business Ownership Basics

Before we can discuss the price and value of a refrigerator *business*, let's talk briefly about the different forms of business ownership. A business can be structured as a sole proprietorship (one owner), a partnership (multiple owners), or a corporation (single or multiple owners). If it's not a corporation, an ownership *certificate* is all that's needed. If it's a corporation, however, ownership is evidenced by *shares of stock*. Each share is legal proof that the holder owns a proportional (or *pro rata*) percentage of the corporation.

The price and number of shares issued varies greatly from one corporation to another. Once the value of a corporation is known—a complex, arduous process, as discussed below—that value is divided by the number of shares issued. For instance, if the value of the corporation is determined to be $10 million, and the company issues one share of stock, then the value of that single share would be $10 million. If, on the other hand, the corporation had one million shares of stock issued, then the value of its stock price would be $10 per share.

The Price & Value of a Refrigerator Company

The principles of value, worth, and price are the same for a *company* that makes refrigerators as they are for the *product* they sell. To reduce costs and shorten manufacturing time, a refrigerator company will develop new, more efficient robotics and automated assembly techniques. It will also develop new accessories and features that add to their products' economic value—increasing their ability to command higher prices. The combination of lower costs and higher product prices enables the company and its salesforce to maintain a profit margin sufficient to stay in business—or even expand. As with any business that continues to remain profitable, the value of that business also rises and results in a higher price at the time the business is sold.

The decision to sell a company is usually motivated by a change in circumstances. The owner of a private company may simply be tired of the responsibility and desirous of a change—or a chance to retire. They may also want to expand or improve the business but need the capital to do so. Whatever the reason, so long as the company has actual value, the owner must come up with a price that both they and a buyer (or buyers) can agree upon. This can happen in different ways:

The Single-Owner Scenario: When a company is sold by one individual to another, the seller upon full payment transfers the number of shares required to represent the entire business. This could be one share or many, as described above, so long as they collectively represent a 100% ownership interest. However, before this can happen, the buyer and seller need to determine the value of the business, to enable them to determine a price to ask for it.

To make this determination, many factors must be considered, such as the type of business, its location, the nature of (and demand for) its products, sales revenue and profit over time, and the likely ability of the business to continue in the future as a profitable enterprise. Often, a smart owner wishing to sell a business will secure the services of a business valuation company to analyze these factors in detail. Once the owner has determined what they believe is a realistic current value for the business, they will then decide on what they feel is a fair price to ask for it and begin looking for a buyer.

A prospective new owner may also wish to secure the services of their own business valuation company—quite often with different conclusions—and propose a different price. Regardless of the business evaluations by either party, the actual price will only be known when a willing seller and a willing buyer have agreed upon an acceptable price for ownership of the business. When the purchase and sale agreement is concluded, the original owner (seller) receives funds from the new owner (buyer) who, in return, receives documents conveying total ownership of the company.

The Multiple-Owner Scenario begins in the same way—with mutual analysis of a company's value and a negotiated agreement on price. When the transaction from one to many owners occurs, the selling shareholder receives full payment for the business from all of the purchasing shareholders and transfers share to the buyers based on their percentage ownership. For instance: one purchaser buying half the corporation and two others each purchasing one-quarter of it. The person buying half the business would get 50% of the issued shares while the two individuals purchasing a quarter of the business would each receive 25% of the shares. So long as the ownership remains private, the number of shares is irrelevant, provided that they can be divided accurately.

The Public-Owner Scenario: If the corporation has decided to have many shareholders, then the initial sale of stock to the public—called the initial public offering or IPO is normally done utilizing the services of an investment banking firm. Such a firm normally assists the corporation in determining its value, and hence the proportional share of the total valuation assigned to each share price. Once the total number of shares being offered for sale by the selling shareholder(s) is concluded the shares are free to trade between shareholders on the open market—normally a stock exchange. Going forward, the share price of the stock will fluctuate in the market based on investor sentiment. Its price will be determined by supply and demand of buyers and sellers, and their differing opinion of the corporation's real value.

The confusion over a company's value and price stems from the fact that shares are traded frequently—sometimes minute by minute—and often with no thought given to the change in corporate valuation between stock transactions. Sometimes a shareholder decides to sell their shares for reasons that have nothing to do with the company's actual valuation. They may need cash today to pay a child's tuition or other similar personal reasons. They may have seen a "sky is falling" headline about the company whose shares they own—or a mistaken rumor about the company inventing a miracle cure. Either reaction would cause the stock price to fall or rise, while the value of the company could remain unchanged.

The price of a stock on any given day at any moment in time, reflects someone's (often many people's) opinion of what they *believe* to be the value of a company. Those beliefs very often have nothing to do with the company's *actual* value—something that can be known only through a labor-intensive analysis process. Most normal people are content to rely on mental shortcuts, gut feelings, and the consensus of others—many of whom are also biased.

It is a mistake to think that others who are buying and selling stocks at a frenetic pace know something you don't. The chances are that they do not. More often than not, they are betting (gambling/speculating) on what they think the price of the stock will be tomorrow, next month, or even next year. The day-to-day price changes of a stock seldom reflect any concerted effort to determine the real value of the enterprise next year or several years hence—the focal point of any serious investor's attention. As we discussed in Chapter 8, the trading habits of typical stock speculators very often result in sub-optimal financial results.

The Price of Stock

Refrigerators and stock portfolios are distinctly different ways to spend money, as we discussed in Chapter 3. One will almost always decline in value over time, while the other has the potential to increase in value. However, they are alike in one respect: their *intrinsic* value and their *economic* value—as measured by assigned worth and price—are not the same.

A company can have ample evidence of its intrinsic value. It may have products or services that people genuinely need and are willing to buy. It may be efficiently run.

It may be out-performing its competition. It may have strong, consistent earnings. If it has all of these things, then it even has a high probability of future success. However, *the company's intrinsic value does not control its perceived economic value*—namely its worth in the eyes of others and the price that others are willing to pay.

The way companies are bought and sold is complicated. The mergers-and-acquisitions process is one approach, but outside most people's means. The other way is the buying and selling of company stock or other financial instruments. A share of stock is literally proof of ownership in part of a company or other entity. Buying and selling shares of a company—the main focus of this book—is where price and value are most frequently confused. Understanding how price and value are *not* the same is a crucial element of successful investment.

Some people like to compare buying and selling stock to gambling on a sporting event or a random number in a drawing. The two are worlds apart. Applying gambling principles to the stock market is dangerous. Speculation—based on normal, Reactive biases—is a key reason why individual investor behavior tends to underperform the market, as discussed in Chapter 8.

The price of stock in a company is not arbitrary; it exists for a reason, usually connected to a business need. For example, to expand or improve the business, a company's owners can raise money (also known as "permanent capital") by selling stock in the company. To do so, they must first establish a price that others are willing to pay.

This involves determining a company's economic value—a complex, data-intensive process. A highly skilled analyst must examine the company's inner workings, history, prospects, and reputation to come up with their best approximation of its *perceived* worth, present and future, to a prospective buyer. Once they assess a company's overall economic value, the expert assigns a defendable *price* to describe its worth.

The initial share price is a simple calculation. Just divide the total price by the number of shares one plans to sell. However, once those shares are publicly available, the share price can vary widely, even though the company's value remains stable. Those considering whether to buy the stock (or the entire company) must make the same basic calculations as the analysts who recommended the initial price. Some will put a great deal of time and energy into the analysis; others will rely on instinct or speculation. In either case, the perceived economic value will vary for everyone, and the price will rise and fall regularly. In theory, a price may coincide exactly with a company's intrinsic value, but most of the time it will not.

A Privately-Owned Company Goes Public
(one owner sells to many shareholders)

Consider a hypothetical example: a small, local grocery store. Started as a family business, the company has gained a reputation for high-quality, organic foods, exceptional service, and community service. For several reasons, the owners decide to offer the company—or at least part of it—for sale.

Following that decision, experts in financial asset pricing are retained to make a formal evaluation. They pore over the books, examining earnings, owned property and other assets, debts, 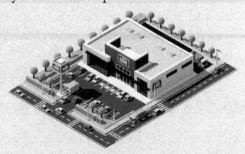 cash on hand, and other variables—over the entire history of the business. They also examine non-financial factors such as location, reputation, management history, and perception in the community. As a result, they make an estimate of the company's probability of success in the future and assign a price to that assessment of worth. For this example, we'll say that price is $25 million.

The original owners now have choices to make. They can offer to sell one share (the entire company) for $25 million, or 25 million shares at $1 each, or something in between. Usually, the share price decision is based on what is normal and acceptable in the market—not so low to be suspect and not so high to be out of reach. So, a typical decision might be to set the price at $25 a share, making the number of shares one million.

At this point, the selling process comes under the same rules that govern the price of milk, or of a refrigerator to keep it in. Buyers will pay what they think the company is worth to them. A large chain may want to buy all the shares—or at least a controlling majority—but offers a different price, based on a different perception of value. Individual share buyers will also have their own views of a company's worth to them. No matter how well-informed or poorly-informed those perceptions of value may be, a buyer or a seller of the company's stock will only pay or accept a price that satisfies that perception.

Once the company's stock is available to be bought and sold, its price will vary from moment to moment—sometimes by large percentages—because perceptions change rapidly and unpredictably. However, the value of the company and its long-term potential for growth will remain constant in the near-term.

We Can't All Be Warren Buffett

Determining the long-term value of a company is an arduous task—one that requires extraordinary skill, focus, and a willingness to devote the majority of one's time and energy to one particular form of wealth—money. The problem is that there are more types of wealth (or "wealths," to coin a new term) besides money. As outlined in the next chapter, non-monetary wealth can be anything of value, including good relationships, fond memories, and the satisfaction of leaving the world a better place than it was. Monetary wealth is a means to those ends, but not an end in itself.

This leaves most of us with a quandary. To create and enjoy non-monetary wealth leaves little time left over to focus on creating monetary wealth with discipline and skill. Even if each of us had the inner capacity to be another Warren Buffett, we simply can't or won't devote the time and effort required to discover the long-term economic value of the companies we buy. Without that knowledge and experience, all we really know is the ever-changing price.

As a result, the vast majority of investors rely on "gut" feelings or mental shortcuts. But our normal, Reactive impulses and cognitive biases are often wrong. When a price suddenly rises or falls, our feelings may induce us to buy or sell without any consideration of the long-term financial results. We also frequently rely on the advice of others—who may have their own agendas or be just as influenced by their cognitive biases about short-term price changes. As we will discussed in Chapter 8, individual investor choices made in this manner nearly always result in poorer financial returns than that of the market as a whole.

Most of us will probably never have the time or ability to "be like Buffett." So, the alternative is to make a simpler decision—one with a high probability of growth in value despite the daily fluctuations of price. Rather than react to short-term market volatility, invest in a large group of the nation's major companies, whose future value is more easily anticipated. Even when an individual company in that group experiences problems—as some certainly will—the likelihood that they will *all* fail is highly improbable. Over the long-term, history has shown that such a strategy has a high probability of success.

Watching the Crops Grow

In 1986, Warren Buffett purchased a 400-acre farm in Nebraska—not knowing a thing about farming. All he knew was how many bushels of corn and soybeans it could produce and what the operating expenses would be. On average, he calculated, it would produce an investment return of 10% and that productivity and prices would probably increase over time. He has never sold the farm. It was a positive albeit small, unremarkable investment.

"After all," Buffett wrote, "if a moody fellow with a farm bordering my property yelled out a price every day to me at which he would either buy my farm or sell me his—and those prices varied widely over short periods of time depending on his mental state—how in the world could I be other than benefited by his erratic behavior? If his daily shout-out was ridiculously low, and I had some spare cash,

I would buy his farm. If the number he yelled was absurdly high, I could either sell to him or just go on farming."

Buffett has only visited the farm twice in over 30 years, but he uses it as an example of how to separate value and price. Rather than react impulsively on erratic price information, he is content with the farm's value and perfectly happy "watching the crops grow," so to speak.

Buffett's long practice of evaluating companies' long-term value—and of buying them in spite of, or more accurately because of panic over falling prices—has made him one of the wealthiest humans on the planet. But he also acknowledges that not everyone can do the same. "You don't need to be an expert in order to achieve satisfactory investment returns," he said. "But if you aren't, you must recognize your limitations and follow a course certain to work reasonably well. Keep things simple and don't swing for the fences. When promised quick profits, respond with a quick 'no.'"

This outlook was expressed in an unusual way at the 2014 annual gathering of Berkshire Hathaway investors. For his eventual heirs (and anyone else who would listen), Buffett endorsed a simple portfolio of low-cost index funds.

Buffett discussed provisions of his will in his annual shareholder letter. Not surprisingly to those who knew him, his Berkshire shares would all go to philanthropic organizations over a 10-year period. But the cash bequest to his wife came with a simple instruction to the trustee: invest 90% in a low-cost S&P 500 index fund. "I believe the trust's long-term results from this policy will be superior to those investors—whether pension funds, institutions, or individuals—who employ high-fee managers," he said.

Arguably, most cannot replicate Buffett's phenomenal success. Very few of us can even benefit from it directly. (Berkshire Hathaway shares now cost over $300,000 each!) However, anyone can take the path he recommended to his own heirs.

Our Reactive, System 1 Problem

Knowing something is true does not always protect us from our impulses. The price of something can be higher or lower than its actual value—sometimes within a very short span of time. If we stop to think, we know that speculating about those changes will likely result in failure. "Half of all coin-flippers will win their first toss," Buffett once quipped. "*None* of those winners has an expectation of profit if he continues to play the game." Despite this obvious fact, we tend to speculate anyway, constantly looking at the scoreboard instead of focusing on the playing field.

Our normal, Reactive brains—reinforced by a constant stream of price information—find it easier to react than to pause and reflect on the long-term probabilities. The pressure to "do something—*anything!*"— is enormous. A few examples from behavioral psychology will illustrate the point:

Priming – Subconscious exposure to an idea primes us to think of an associated idea and to act accordingly. Today's news is overwhelmingly saturated with how stock prices are changing, with green up arrows and red down arrows always in the display. When the number (up or down) is large enough, it becomes an urgent story. The frequency of such news increases this subconscious bias. Emotionally focused on today's price shift, we find it difficult to pause and reflect on anything long-term.

Cognitive Ease – Things that are familiar or simpler seem truer than things that require hard thought or are more difficult to see. The difference between price and value is unfamiliar territory for many, so we are more likely to take the simpler route and consider only today's price. When an undue focus on price is championed by someone we trust—a family member or a purported expert—the wrong choice can seem even easier. Our affinity for the source of information, however flawed, makes it easier to focus on the wrong thing.

The Law of Small Numbers – Our brains have difficulty with statistics; we greatly prefer small, easily comprehended numbers. A momentary change in an index price is easier to grasp than a long-term, overall growth trend, so it is difficult to focus on the latter.

The Availability Bias – When asked to estimate a numeric event—like the value of our portfolio tomorrow—the ease with which we can retrieve information influences our answer. A change in a stock price is immediately known, especially if we've set an alert on our smartphones. Whatever the change, it is psychologically easier to respond to it than to pause and reflect on the long-term probabilities. Also, whenever we've experienced an emotional trauma—in person or vicariously—from a recent economic downturn, an overreaction is even easier.

Loss Aversion – As a rule, normal people tend to work harder to avoid losses than to achieve gains. The fear of regret over having bought or sold a stock too soon—or too late—is a powerful emotional response to changing prices. Too often, this emotion prevents us from even considering the bigger picture.

The Herd Mentality – Our subconscious, emotional responses are often tied to what we see others doing. We crave recognition and respect, which makes it difficult to resist following others in their speculative behavior. Without a practiced habit of keeping price changes at arm's length, we are more likely to follow the lead of those around us.

Fortunately, it is also possible for normal people to recognize and overcome these biases. When it comes to the critical decisions of value and price, we can develop practices that will curb our impulses to spill our financial wealth.

Investorship Strategies and Habits

Reactive, System 1 impulses are a part of what economist John Maynard Keynes called our "animal spirits," the instincts and emotions that influence and guide human behavior. For example, he held that people's positive economic activities were more about spontaneous optimism than they were about mathematical expectations. Since Keynes' time, behavioral economists have shown how much our non-analytical nature can govern decisions affecting wealth. However, although these impulses are strong—and perfectly normal—we are not helpless when we make spending and investment decisions.

The principles of Investorship hold that our normal, Reactive impulses on spending can be curtailed with practice and patience. When it comes to the issues of price and value, a good first step is to think about everyday examples. Remembering how price and value are not related in everyday life will help when you are faced with unfamiliar investment decisions.

An Unlikely Scenario

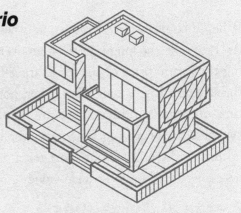

Imagine living in a house or condominium that you own—either outright or with the help of a mortgage. Despite its imperfections, it is home. It satisfies many basic needs and, in all probability, will appreciate in value over time.

Now imagine a stranger coming to your door, offering you money for the house or condo right now. If his price is ridiculously low, you will probably close the door—and perhaps call the police (or suggest counseling). If it is ridiculously high, you might accept it as a windfall—if he is not actually mad. But if the price is anywhere in between, you will almost certainly just say no. You were not considering selling and are satisfied with your home and the likelihood of its increased value in the future. It has value worth more to you than any price he is likely to offer. Price is wholly irrelevant, and you would consider anyone offering to buy suspicious.

Now, relate that unlikely scenario to investments. If a stock or fund has value in the long term, and you have no immediate need to sell it, then almost no price will be acceptable. However, with investments there *is* a "stranger at the door" quoting a different price every day. Whether it's a mobile investment app, a too-frequent portfolio review, or a cocktail party conversation, the price message is persistent, and almost always unrelated to a portfolio's long-term value.

The secret is to treat the "stranger at the door" with the same suspicion when it comes to the price of stocks as you would with an uninvited offer to buy your house. The stranger may not be deranged, but his message is almost always moot. If you have no immediate need to sell something of value, then almost no price is worthwhile.

When it comes to investments, another way to "tame our animal spirits" is to take the longer view about everything. If the process of guessing the future price of a stock share is futile, then don't waste time in the attempt. Life is too full of other, non-monetary "wealths" to spend time on what is ultimately a coin toss. Instead, with the limited time available for acquiring monetary wealth—a worthy goal—ignore or minimize the noise about short-term price changes and instead make decisions based on long-term value.

Practical Guidelines

There are several simple changes in attitude that normal people can adopt when it comes to buying and selling stocks:

Don't wait for the "right moment." – Always remember that, in hindsight, *everything* you do as an investor can be viewed as having been wrong: If you buy a stock and it immediately goes down, you were wrong for buying it. If you buy a stock and it immediately goes up, then you were wrong for not having bought more. If you sell a stock and it immediately goes up some more, you were wrong for having sold it. If you sell it and it immediately goes down, you were wrong for not shorting the stock (a technique that allows you to make money when a stock price declines).

So, since everything you do can be seen in hindsight as having been wrong, the key is not to look back and second guess a decision that was well-reasoned, sensibly executed, and intelligently acquired. Instead, turn your attention to your next well-reasoned investment. Any moment is appropriate when an investment has value—and a high probability of growth over the long term.

Turn down the noise. – It is impossible to exclude all "news" about the price of stocks. However, you should learn to recognize it for what it is—noise. You should review your portfolio, of course, but only occasionally. Some adjustments are inevitable. But for the vast majority of investors a daily or hourly update on stock prices is irrelevant at best. At worst, it stimulates our Reactive nature to make impulsive decisions. Limit your daily diet of noise about price changes, which will blind us to the true, long-term value of our investments.

Keep it to yourself. – True wealth, both monetary and non-monetary, is inconspicuous. Conspicuous consumption is not a true indicator of wealth. In fact, it is often evidence of financial "spilling" and forfeiture of greater wealth. So, when a stock price increases or decreases—as it usually will—a savvy investor will seldom openly call attention to his or her decisions. Bragging about price—an unpredictable, largely irrelevant event—will invariably be followed by reasons to regret bragging. When it comes to value, confidence—in both monetary and non-monetary wealth decisions—is its own reward.

The secret to ignoring price and focusing on value is to master the "art of the shrug." While it is prudent to know *how* one has invested—based on a high likelihood of increased value—a calm indifference to the noise of price changes is invaluable. The ability to shrug provides an emotional insulation against the heat and noise of daily distractions. In the words of the British admonition on the eve of the Blitz, we need to "Keep Calm and Carry On."

Always recognize the impossibility of trying to predict the short-term price changes that will occur regularly in the financial markets. Remember that NO ONE can predict the unpredictable. Those who believe they can do so are delusional, ignorant, or a combination of the two. A better option is not to try. It will only exhaust, frustrate, and disillusion you. It will dampen your ability to recognize real opportunity, spend carefully (with less spilling), and allocate sufficient spending to appreciable assets. By refusing to play the price guessing game, you will become able to diversify yourself wisely among many wealths.

Asking Questions

Before moving on to Chapter 6—on the nature of wealth—ask yourself the following question on the subject of price and value:

What price would you be willing to pay for full, legal ownership of one acre of land in a swamp? What questions would you ask before offering that price?

In Chapter 10, there are other questions about price and value designed to help you pause, reflect, and engage your Reflective, System 2 faculties on this subject.

IDENTIFY THE FINANCIALLY SUCCESSFUL PERSON

*"Hey, buddy, can you lend me ten bucks
for my valet parking?"*

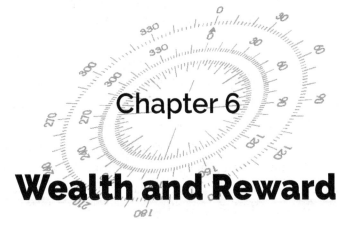

Chapter 6

Wealth and Reward

"Too many people spend money they haven't earned, to buy things they don't want, to impress people that they don't like."
— Will Rogers

In Dubai, United Arab Emirates, a curious fad has emerged. In exclusive restaurants, you can order almost any kind of food or drink with a spectacular added ingredient: *gold*. On burgers and fries, entrées, desserts, and on cappuccinos or non-alcoholic beverages, flakes, coatings, or infusions of pure gold are liberally applied and presumably consumed. Eating gold purportedly does no harm, but it does provide a display of conspicuous consumption—literally. (It also gives an odd new meaning to the saying, "put your money where your mouth is.")

This odd practice has spread to other parts of the world. It may say something about modern society, but it also begs the question at the heart of this book. What is wealth, why do we want it, how do we get it, and how do we retain it?

What Is Wealth?

Wealth signifies an abundance of something of value. But the word itself conjures a wide range of emotions and mental images. It comes from the Middle English "welthe" or "weolthe," meaning happiness or prosperity. Today, it can express negatives like social inequality and conspicuous consumption. It also has positive associations like comfort, security, and well-being. In general, we want to have it, but many of us don't have a clear definition of what wealth actually *is*. Neither do the gold-eaters in Dubai or those who envy or resent them.

Wealth, or prosperity, is about more than money or the things we buy with it. To be wealthy includes higher aspirations like generosity, social connection, exploration, and self-expression. Good health, personal satisfaction, and good memories are also essential to the concept of prosperity. And wealth is also associated with your reputation or position of influence. But money is still essential. Financial wealth—the subject of this book—is fundamental to attaining many of the things we associate with being wealthy.

Of course, some intangible forms of wealth are attainable *without* the use of money, or without large amounts of it. A Buddhist monk or other unworldly person can be said to have great spiritual wealth. True practitioners of simple lifestyles also experience a measure of wealth unknown to conspicuous consumers. However, even these wise or fortunate individuals have needs that must be met by the use of money. At the end of the day, our "net worth" as humans still involves a curious collection of needs, admirable qualities, and life experiences. Attaining most of these requires a sufficient quantity of spendable wealth.

Who Is Wealthy?

Mere financial capital does not make a person wealthy. A useful way to understand true wealth is to look at those who really have it—and those who only think they do. We'll start with the latter.

One example is a lottery winner who has received an unexpected (and wildly unlikely) influx of cash. All too often, he or she begins spending that money on expensive things that make them more conspicuous to those around them—creating an illusion of wealth. In their minds, other perceptions are paramount. The combination of conspicuous consumption, and even acts of fraud to help maintain that conspicuous consumption, too often results in total loss of the money and can lead to moral and legal jeopardy.

Another example, convicted Tyco CEO Dennis Koslowski, infamously spent $6,000 on a shower curtain, $2,000 on a trash can, and over $2 million on his wife's birthday party. The only way to sustain such extravagant spending involved widespread accounting fraud that eventually alerted the SEC and led to fines, restitution, and a prison term.

The lottery winner who loses everything, and the CEO who commits fraud to sustain their conspicuous consumption, do so because they lack *non-monetary capital*. Such capital includes qualities such as motivation, an appropriate level of knowledge and understanding, wisdom, and discipline. Those possessing these qualities are often known for their long-term vision and creativity, their ability to see things in context, and their patience in the face of adversity. As a general rule of wealth, those who develop sufficient levels of non-monetary capital tend to be successful in generating and sustaining greater financial capital.

This doesn't mean those lacking these qualities are unintelligent. It simply means that their unconscious bias towards conspicuous consumption has precluded a more thoughtful, System 2 approach to spending and meeting genuine needs over time.

Fortunately, there are also examples of those who possess significant non-monetary capital and are consequently financially wealthy. Businessman-entrepreneur Warren Buffet has shown great capacity for long-term thinking, weighing consequences, and deferring short-term gratification. The "big picture" quality of his prosperity includes the fact that he famously strives to give much of it away—often through the philanthropic efforts of others who possess significant non-monetary capital.

Such qualities are attainable by everyone. But that poses a quandary. Even when we know that wealth is about more than just money, we still need to spend it throughout our lives. Monetary wealth—the means to higher, more aspirational goals—is the very thing we always seem to lack in sufficient quantity. Or at least we *think* we lack it. Our normal, Reactive, often unconscious perceptions may be preventing a more thoughtful view of our actual wealth potential.

Magnifying Your Earnings

One reason we have a hard time visualizing our own wealth—and our potential for investing—is our System 1 habit of focusing only on the present. We fail to see our lifetime earnings potential.

Take Jay Williams, for example. At 25 years old, he has a modest annual salary of $35,000. If you assume an annual salary increase of 5% for 40 years—until retirement at age 65—then Jay's gross accumulated earnings, before inflation, will add up to over $6.6 million. This might come as a surprise to most of us, including Jay. It's hard to imagine, especially if we are overly focused on the present.

Now, take a moment to relish that number as if you were in Jay's shoes. It feels good but remember that *it will all be spent* over the same 40-year period, as discussed in Chapter 3. But it's not a futile exercise. A significant portion of that amount can be *magnified* by using Investorship habits:

Take half of Jay's first-year raise. Instead of spending it on a fancier vacation, assume he will invest that same amount in a no-commission, index fund with an average, long-term growth rate of 10%. If Jay continues to invest half of his raise each year, his cumulative investment will be over $110,845, but the cumulative investment gains will likely be over $414,120. That means his total accumulated investment (adjusted for inflation) *would likely be over $524,965!*

In the first case, Jay's accumulated earnings will be impressive but offer nothing to show for 40 years of spending. In the second, the magnification of his earnings means he will likely have a substantial sum available at age 65. Combined with other results of Investorship spending, his wealth will be substantial

Even with such a striking example of future accumulated wealth, it's hard for many to see beyond the immediate need—consumption—and adopt practices that result in greater monetary wealth over time.

Our understanding of wealth is limited by our tendency to view things in the short term. We see present-day examples of conspicuous consumption on the street, in the media, and in the unending stream of ads. These reinforce a notion of wealth based on things that do not retain value. We cannot see the future—no one can. As a result, the potential for predictable, sustainable wealth seems less real.

This takes us back to the previous discussion of what is normal. As with other matters, we tend to favor our intuitive, *Reactive* (System 1) feelings about wealth over our *Reflective* (System 2) ability to pause, reflect, and reason about it.

How We Feel About Wealth

We unconsciously measure wealth by the thing money proverbially can't buy: happiness. We gauge it by our health, our pleasant memories, our cherished possessions, and our personal relationships. As we discussed in the previous chapter, those things can be perfectly valid needs. But they are ends or goals, not the means of meeting those needs. With barter long out of fashion, money is the only practical way to reliably measure our present or potential future wealth.

But it's not that simple. When it comes to making decisions affecting wealth, our human, *subjective* perceptions have enormous influence. Kahneman himself demonstrated this in his Nobel prize-winning work on prospect theory. *We are prone to making wealth decisions based on preconceptions of immediate emotional impact—regardless of the actual, provable outcome.*

We tend to over-rely on subjective feelings when it comes to wealth. Mere changes or fluctuations in wealth *seem* more important than its long-term value. This can be the case even when the subjective experience is unfounded or misleading. We are emotionally averse to loss, even when that loss is demonstrably a short-term phenomenon.

We are also remarkably sensitive to *relative* changes in wealth. Losing or gaining $100 seems way more important when starting with $200 than it does when starting with $2,000.

Wealth is an objective reality governed by our subjective perceptions. We either have enough money to satisfy needs and wants or we do not, but our feelings on the matter are more complex and can affect our actions—not always for the better.

Consume: Now or Later?

Our perceptions govern the two different modes of spending. One is for immediate consumption, on things that may be necessary or useful—or at least gratifying—but that will invariably decrease in value. The other is for *future* consumption, on things that will likely increase in value, even though they are less likely to be noticed. They represent *future* wealth. A new car—something that can be seen in the present—will only depreciate. However, a portfolio—typically unseen, unless you're prone to bragging—will likely increase in value, making it more likely that you can have that car in the future. That type of appreciating wealth is *convertible* into future wealth.

However, our Reactive, System 1 impulses make it difficult to choose convertible wealth over immediate consumption. We are prone to seeing the immediate need as more pressing than the future potential, and too often sacrifice it.

The Marshmallow Metaphor

In a well-known experiment conducted in the late 1960s, Stanford psychologist Walter Mischel studied the behavior of children faced with a choice between immediate and delayed gratification.

Given the choice between a small treat now or two small treats if they waited fifteen minutes, the children behaved in different ways. Some ate one marshmallow immediately while others waited—with effort—for the promised two marshmallows. The subject's age often affected the results.

Some have argued whether or not Mischel's experiment correlates with later success or failure in life, or whether some people are better at delayed gratification than others. But the bigger point is that we can easily identify with the kids in the test, especially (in my case) when writing about this example right before dinner.

Taking the first marshmallow right now is a great metaphor for spending on immediate consumption. It's at the heart of the "spilling" phenomenon described in Chapter 3. It's also a very normal aspect of human nature—even when we know it will limit our future consumption.

Waiting fifteen minutes for two marshmallows is also a metaphor—for spending towards long-term growth. Like the children in the marshmallow experiment, we need to develop habits that reinforce reasoning and increase the likelihood of spending behavior that leads to future, spendable wealth.

Choosing to spill our wealth for short-term consumption is rooted in Reactive biases and thinking errors. One of these is *cognitive ease*. Consuming something immediately is a familiar activity. It's easy, natural, and perfectly normal. So, *it seems truer* than something novel, hard to imagine, or requiring thought or reflection—like the abstract notion of future wealth. Advertisers and retail marketers know this well when they display candy and gossip magazines prominently at the check-out line (or perhaps more accurately, the "checked-out" line.) This can blind us to the lost potential that spilling represents.

To justify a consume-now decision, we also tell ourselves stories that we believe to be true. This habit, called *associative coherence*, leads us to make unwarranted associations between events, circumstances, and occurrences. Our minds naturally draw false conclusions, such as believing that conspicuous consumption of new cars or gold-encrusted steaks is somehow proof of wealth rather than the opposite.

We also engage in *substitution*, answering a simpler (usually simplistic) question than the harder one actually required by the circumstances. Instead of grappling with "What will this decision mean for my financial wealth 20 years from now?" we ask, "What will my peers think about me in this new car?" Like other Reactive habits, it makes a life decision seem easier but actually does the opposite.

Inconspicuous Wealth

To offset our normal, short-term attitudes about wealth, we must learn that actual wealth is by definition inconspicuous, if not invisible to outward appearances. Wealth is a combination of:

- *sound principles,*
- *the right ingredients, and*
- *sufficient time to produce the intended results.*

The last point is extremely important, as we will explore later in the book. Wealth seldom if ever occurs immediately or even visibly. Pre-occupation with the outward appearance of wealth is usually an indicator of someone who possesses an oversized ego—of someone nowhere near as wealthy as they hope others perceive them. In fact, the focus on outward appearance indicates the *opposite* of wealth.

For example, consider a soon-to-be-obsolete accessory: the wristwatch. A well-made, generic watch tells the time, and perhaps the date. On the other hand (figuratively, not literally), a Rolex "tells" something else. The price of a Rolex ranges from a few thousand dollars to over $17,000. By spending that amount, wearers accept the notion, reinforced by years of brand marketing, that a Rolex is evidence of great wealth, status, and success. The brand name itself is synonymous with conspicuous consumption and prestige.

Both the Rolex and a high-quality but generic watch are durable, well-designed, comfortable to wear, reasonably attractive, and of course accurate and convenient. However, the Rolex represents a *spilling* of money, as we learned in Chapter 3. The spilling is not just the enormous price differential, but the future wealth forfeited by not following Investorship principles with that money.

Ostentatious display is not only an indicator of the lack of wealth, it can also be the cause of its destruction, as in the earlier example of lottery winners and their excessive spending on luxury items. They *feel* wealthy in the moment because their Reactive tendencies are fully deployed. But too often their financial wealth—mainly things that decline in value—is dissipated and those same Reactive impulses prevent them from securing actual, long-term, appreciating wealth. A better model involves wealth that is inconspicuous, and even boring.

The Frugal Billionaire

Lifestyles of the rich and famous are a mainstay of reality *(sic.)* television. What rich people buy is considered both glamorous and unattainable by mere mortals. However, there are notable exceptions. The third richest man on earth—Warren Buffett—is notoriously *not* a conspicuous consumer.

Aside from the purchase of a private jet—or rather a private jet

Photo by Mark Hirschey, CC BY-SA 2.0

operator, NetJets—Buffett is known for his frugality. He lives in the same house he bought in 1958, buys meals at McDonalds (sometimes with coupons), wears suits by a once unknown designer, drives the same car for years, and sports an $18-dollar haircut.

Buffett's lifestyle is an example of how wealth and visible consumption are not invariably connected. But his wealth is attributable to much more than his frugality. (Many of his beliefs about long-term thinking and investment are manifestations of the Investorship principles put forward in this book.)

An example of inconspicuous, boring, but ultimately prolific wealth is the stock portfolio. If you make regular contributions to an index fund, almost no one will notice. Contrast that with the attention you could expect by spending the same amounts on fancier cars, prestigious watches, designer clothes, or lavish vacations. However, the portfolio typically generates actual results while the glamorous alternative does not. Even attempts to make a portfolio more exciting or brag-worthy—by engaging in day-to-day tinkering with individual stocks—will almost always result in lower returns, as we will see in Chapter 8.

The feelings of excitement or pride instilled by conspicuous spending behavior—on luxury goods, private airplanes, or even in cocktail party bragging about your too-frequent trading—are invariably false indicators. Real wealth, fueled by your non-monetary capital, is unobtrusive but ultimately powerful and sustainable.

Wealth and Investorship

As any good vintner will tell you, good wine is the result of sound principles and practices, the right conditions and ingredients, and time. These in turn will enhance the wine's reputation and, in the hands of competent marketers, generate more demand and a higher price.

However, the reverse is not true. A prestigious brand label may or may not represent a wine producer of the highest standards. But the brand itself—and the price of that brand—are not a guarantee of quality or value.

Tasting the Difference

In 2008, critic Robin Goldstein released a book based on a double-blind experiment published in the *Journal of Wine Economics*. From the over 6,000 observations, researchers concluded that individuals who were unaware of the price did not derive more enjoyment from more expensive wine. In fact, some groups found less enjoyment from more expensive wines.

Another test, also by the American Association of Wine Economists, revealed that people assigned a higher rating to a wine when they were informed—before the tasting—that it

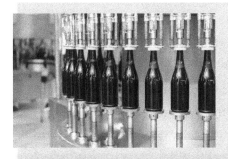 sold for $40 a bottle. Clearly, our preconceptions affect our perceptions.

If quality and price are not connected, then why do people buy $300-dollar bottles of wine? One explanation is that the display of higher spending is erroneously associated with greater wealth. In fact, both affordable and expensive wines can provide comparable pleasure. The latter is, unfortunately, a symptom of spilled wealth.

When asked what it takes to become an investor, the answer most people give is "money." In fact, the real answer involves the five qualities of Investorship. Money, or financial capital (#6), is the natural outcome—not the prerequisite—of following these principles.

Motivation—the desire to achieve a specific, quantifiable, financial goal—may seem obvious, but it must be accompanied by the desire to do so by spending differently, on things that will increase in value.

1. Motivation
2. Knowledge & Understanding
3. Skills
4. Wisdom
5. Discipline

6. Money

Knowledge & Understanding must be specific and limited to what really needs to be known. It is possible to know too much detail—about a company, for example—to the extent it will keep you from acting.

Skills are the subject of later chapters, and are summarized in Appendix A. Such skills are not overly complicated. It is far easier to understand the mechanics of investing in the right index fund—and leave it there for the long term, with only occasional review—than it is to tinker with your portfolio on a frequent basis. As we will see in Chapter 5, such tinkering typically leads to under-performance.

Wisdom is derived from the continuous application of Reflective, System 2-based knowledge and skills, reinforced by the steady but typically boring and inconspicuous accumulation of money.

Discipline is perhaps the most critical quality. A major component of wise spending is time—allowing long-term growth to occur without interruption. It requires discipline and patience to ignore "breaking news" of a short-term stock decline and resist the temptation to sell. This is something our Reflective reasoning understands, but which is always under siege by immediate circumstances. Sometimes, the secret lies in finding ways to short-circuit temptation.

Money, or financial capital, is the happy result of application of the previous five principles. Over time, the habits of Investorship will become part of our Reactive responses, enabling us to make the correct choices with less mental effort.

Lashing Yourself to the Mast

In 2013, Harvard Economics Professor David Laibson used a metaphor from Homer's Odyssey—where Ulysses tied himself to the mast of his boat to resist the Sirens' tempting calls—to illustrate a significant threat to wealth. In this case, the temptation is to spend too easily what we have invested for the long term.

Laibson posed the notion that an enemy of long-term wealth building was the liquidity of today's investments. "In the realm of retirement saving, we have 401(k)s and IRAs where the money is basically liquid," he said, pointing out that with little or no penalty, investors could withdraw funds for many reasons, ultimately sacrificing long-term growth.

Laibson noted that every year, over $100 billion "leaks out" from such accounts before the holders reach retirement. He proposed an alternative, giving people the option to decide how much liquidity they want—choosing to "lash themselves to the mast" for a percentage of their accounts.

In Investorship terms, when the temptation to spend (spill) occurs, the investor has already chosen to stay with their Reflective principles and limited his or her ability to succumb to the Siren call of Reactive impulses.

Laibson's solution—mandatory restraints and related changes in the laws governing retirement accounts—are specific to one form of investment. In fact, voluntary, irrevocable restraint would be a good thing, but investors should also find other ways to "lash themselves to the mast." As we will explore, there are other, more positive ways to give investments the time they require. Besides limiting our ability to spill, we must remind ourselves of the amount of wealth already accumulated and (more importantly) the vast amount of wealth represented by the passage of time.

The Reward

Ultimately, wealth is a reward for your labors, and an assurance that both present and future needs can be met. Money is the means of doing so, but money is not the sole component of wealth. Rather, our core values—our store of non-monetary capital—dictate that we broaden our notion of wealth to include intangible, sometime unglamorous goals that meet our own needs as well as those of others.

A shallow notion of wealth—the possession of highly-visible, status-oriented objects that decline in value—must be replaced by an Investorship model. This means our spending must include a large proportion of assets that *increase* in value. These are usually inconspicuous, if not invisible.

In today's consumer culture, this basic concept seems strange. But in order to spend your way to wealth, you must be able to apply the same practices involved in making fine wine: sound principles, the right ingredients, and time.

Asking Questions

Before moving on to Chapter 7—on the nature of risk—ask yourself the following question on the subject of wealth:

What amount of non-monetary wealth (experiences, relationships, etc.) do you need in order to lead a satisfactory life?

In Chapter 10, there are other questions about wealth designed to help you pause, reflect, and engage your Reflective, System 2 faculties on this subject.

"So, you say you're risk-averse and yet you drove here?"

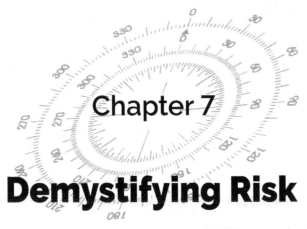

Chapter 7

Demystifying Risk

"Life is inherently risky. There is only one big risk you should avoid at all costs, and that is the risk of doing nothing."
— Denis Waitley

In the late 1860s, U.S. Secretary of State William H. Seward took a calculated risk: he purchased over 14 million acres of arctic land from the Russian Empire. Opponents derided the plan as "Seward's Folly."

They believed it was too risky, the land too barren and distant, the potential benefits too uncertain. They felt the money (over $7 million) could be better spent elsewhere. Seward and his allies took the long view, calculating that the land would become immensely valuable to the country over the coming decades. Seward was correct. The benefits far outweighed the risk. The land became a rich U.S. territory, and is now the great state of Alaska.

Broadly defined, risk is an action or omission whose consequences or outcomes are uncertain. While the concept is easy to define, it is harder to fully understand. It's also difficult to understand our unconscious biases against risk. After all, they are unconscious. But once we come to understand these biases, it becomes easier to manage them when it comes to spending, investment, and wealth.

Everything people do—or fail to do—involves risk. There is no absolute certainty about anything; most outcomes are *possible*. The tricky part is that outcomes are either more or less *probable*. When people fail to consider the element of probability, especially over long periods of time, the result is an unconsciously flawed attitude about risk.

Taking Risks Is Necessary—and Normal

Humans are a risk-taking species. Prehistoric men and women made enormously risky decisions. Going out to hunt for food carried a greater-than-zero chance of *becoming* food for a fellow predator. But these risks were well worth the reward, namely survival and, ultimately, an improvement in their lot. They knew the probability of becoming lunch for a lion, but they also knew the higher probability of starving if we stayed in the cave. So, humans developed ways of evaluating and mitigating dangerous situations. For the most part, we succeeded. The fact that you're here, reading this book, is proof that our prehistoric ancestors learned how to take risks, successfully manage them, and realize their benefits.

Every day, modern-day humans take risks far more complex than those of our ancestors. As life becomes more technologically advanced, people take more risks. Some, like driving a car, involve a probability of a bad outcome to life or health. Others, like engaging with social media, involve a probability of a bad social outcome—or a loss of privacy. Risks can be personal, relational, societal, vocational, or political. And of course, risks can also be financial in nature. Whenever someone decides to spend (or not spend) money, the outcome is uncertain. There is always a probability that something good or bad will result. It may improve or impair our financial situation—our ability to meet our needs—both now and in the future.

Willingness to take risks is considered a virtue if the risks are taken with understanding and forethought. Most people would approve of a risk-taker who weighs probable outcomes, considers the likelihood of benefits, and takes reasonable precautions. When the risk is understood and familiar—like driving a car—most people think it's perfectly normal and give very little thought to the risk factor. Like our ancestors, normal human beings make calculations and decisions that will likely, but not with absolute certainty, make the risk worth taking.

For some reason, the acceptance of reasonable amounts of risk often does not seem to apply to matters involving financial investment. The thought of investing in a volatile market poses a risk that some people are unwilling or unable to take. Our *Reactive* (System 1) fear of financial loss and fear of regretting one's actions overwhelm the conscious, *Reflective* (System 2) reasoning process—preventing us from acting (or refraining from action) in our own, long-term interests.

A Failure of Understanding

When it comes to financial investments, many people define themselves as being "risk averse" without knowing why they believe this. This is a profoundly flawed view, and one that often results in spilling—the unwitting forfeiture of future wealth. Evidence of this unconscious bias can be found in people's overuse of what we will call *(un)truisms*. Like all generalizations, the results of believing in (un)truisms are not absolute but are useful in defining the problem.

(UN)TRUISM	RESULTS
"What goes up must come down."	If viewed only in the short term, this infers, falsely, that *everything* can be lost if the price of an investment declines to (or below!) the original price.
"Don't invest more than you can afford to lose."	Again, if applied only to a short-term view, this results in exceedingly unnecessary caution and timidity.
"Buy low; sell high"	With only the immediate situation in mind, adherents to this view tend to dodge and swerve to avoid immediate, perceived threats—ignoring long-term probabilities and typically spilling unnecessarily. (See Chapter 8.)

Risk aversion in financial matters—particularly regarding invest-ments—stems from a short-term view of losses and gains, and from a failure to see probable value increases over time. For example, people see a precipitous drop in the S&P 500—made to seem worse by the way most stock prices are visually graphed. This generates a strong, Reactive, gut feeling of fear or anxiety. Without a long-term perspec-tive, a common, normal reaction is to sell (making the short-term situation even worse). This forfeits the future value of an otherwise strong, long-term investment. It also reinforces the feeling that risk is something to be avoided at all costs.

If this "risk averse" behavior was applied to other types of risk—like driving a car—it would be considered odd or eccentric. When some-one drives to the store for a quart of ice cream, there is a remote chance you will die or be injured on the way. There are comparable risks in eating a meal or taking a shower. But those risks—however real—do not prevent us from taking them. Most people take reasonable precau-tions to reduce those probabilities—or purchase insurance to mitigate the small but real chance of a bad outcome. Above all, people take risks because the potential, highly probable benefits—enjoyment of ice cream, a meal, or good hygiene—far outweigh the probability of a bad outcome.

The peculiar aversion to investment risk is understandable. Unlike driving a car, most people have not become accustomed to consciously evaluating probable, long-term results. For example, an index fund—representing the top companies as measured by their market capi-talization—has an enormously high probability of growth over time. However, that same fund may show dramatic changes from day to day and will frequently drop in price for short periods of time. There is a statistically greater probability that investors will lose money—*if* they buy or sell in response to those short-term changes. But as his-torical trends show, the probability of a positive outcome increases dramatically over a longer period of time. Although success is never a certainty, the risk is substantially less than that of everyday activities like driving a car.

When these factors are weighed, the risk involved in investment is relative, but people are conditioned to think it is not. The news media—usually for ratings reasons—are adept at highlighting the short-term volatility of the market. One-day or one-week declines involving big numbers are presented as frightening narratives, feeding the myth of high risk. But when people bother to look at the actual, long-term benefits and weigh them against the diminishing probability of loss over time, the narrative changes. It may be boring in the world of 24-hour news, but it is ultimately positive for the investor who has learned to evaluate and tolerate risk.

Why Do Normal People Fear Risk?

When it comes to investing, risk-aversion is a normal but ultimately self-destructive behavior. Too often, people are focused on the immediate situation and do not sufficiently consider the probability of outcomes over the long term. They fail to weigh probable outcomes along with the likely benefits. In an unfamiliar and uncertain environment, they let their Reactive feelings take control rather than pause, reflect, and manage the situation.

A major cause of this behavior is the fear of regret. Regret and embarrassment—unlike many other negative emotions—can be experienced anew just by recalling the past experience. Because that feeling is so unpleasant, the normal response is to avoid thinking about the past mistakes that trigger them. Unfortunately, this keeps people from learning and acting differently.

Some regrets are more powerful than others. According to many psychologists, people tend to feel greater regret when bad outcomes result from *action* (commission) than when they result from *inaction* (omission). They also tend to frame situations narrowly, avoiding actions seen as risky in a single, isolated situation without considering other, related situations in context—and over time.

Narrow Framing and Perceived Risk

In his book, *Thinking, Fast and Slow*, Daniel Kahneman describes an investor who has a choice of selling one of two stocks in order to cover the cost of his daughter's wedding. One stock is currently priced higher than when he originally bought it—and therefore identified as a "winner" in his mind.

 The other is currently priced lower than when it was originally purchased and is therefore considered a "loser." Which stock is he more likely to sell?

He has two choices. He can give himself pleasure by selling the "winner" and boosting his prowess as a savvy investor. Or he can cause himself pain by selling the "loser," admitting defeat—an action he will deeply regret. Based on this narrow, short-term perception of the risk, he notes that he would probably sell the "winner"—choosing pleasure over pain. Many other normal people would do the same.

However, a Reflective, System 2-based approach would likely result in the opposite decision. Using this system, he would keep the value and long-term growth potential of the whole portfolio paramount in his mind and would avoid the temptation to separate individual stocks into misleadingly labeled (winner/loser) mental accounts. Therefore, if any stock had to be sold—to meet a legitimate financial need—it should be the one with a lower potential performance level over time.

Such a decision is not automatic, of course. A stock that is priced lower than when it was originally bought is not necessarily destined to underperform, nor is the higher-priced stock destined to succeed in the long term. However, if such

> a spending choice is unavoidable, the decision should be based on a broad framing of the facts, not on a narrowly-defined perception of emotional risk.

This explains why so many people are daunted by short-term failure in the market—or even by hearing others' accounts of stock-trading misfortune. The loss from selling a stock that has declined produces greater regret than doing nothing during the same period. As a result, people are reluctant to even enter the market. If they do, they tend to react to what their emotions mislead them to think are unacceptable risks.

Normal, Reactive responses, fueled by lack of understanding and amplified by a hyperbolic media, deter us from taking reasonable risks and consciously adopting a calm, long-term view of the process.

The Roller Coaster Phenomenon

Another factor that leads to risk aversion is market volatility (wide swings in either direction). Financial news is filled with stories of how an individual stock price—or an entire index fund—rose or fell dramatically that day or week. Price performance over a short period of time is portrayed as something of great significance. Such news stories are amplified by people's craving for "instant news alerts" of price changes, which incessantly pop up on customized mobile apps.

A dramatic-looking stock price rise or fall may be factually accurate, but it is completely beside the point. Unless someone needs to sell for some external reason, a scary price drop should never occasion a decision to sell. (Those who do won't be the first. By the time the price plunges, it's already too late.)

Our intuitive, Reactive sensibilities tend to prefer small numbers and simple conclusions over larger numbers and complex calculations. Our brains have a difficult time with statistics. According to a phenomenon called the "law of small numbers," people tend to affirm conclusions based on small sample sizes, even though data from larger samples are more accurate.

This all-too-human failing is true in many areas, including opinion polling, where a small number of respondents can produce results that are dramatic—and widely believed—but are false or misleading. But this bias also happens when we project the wrong meaning to rapidly rising or falling stock prices. Our "sampling size" problem in this case is the number of years over which the change occurs. During a period of 0.04 years (slightly over two weeks), the price of an index fund may decline dramatically—as the S&P 500 has done on many occasions. However, if the basis period changes from 0.04 years to 40 years, growth is reliably positive.

In short, our natural, Reactive perceptions of risk tend to be misleading, especially when we have not internalized the big picture. Over any given short period of time, the financial markets are indeed volatile. However, the actual, historical data indicate that long-term investment—in the right index fund (see Appendix A)—carries far less risk than driving a car.

Perhaps a good way to conclude the roller coaster analogy is to look at the risk involved in actually riding one. Industry statistics place the risk of injury from roller coasters at one in 24 million, and the risk of death at one in 750 million. While a bad outcome is theoretically *possible*, it is not at all *probable*. The same attitude toward risk should be applied to our investment decisions.

No Guarantees

Humans love the notion of certainty, or at least the feeling of it. The world is filled with uncertain possibilities, so it is comforting to think of something as certain, even if it's not. This results in a phenomenon known as the "zero-risk bias." This means people tend to prefer approaches that completely eliminate *some* risks even though the alternative would produce a greater *overall* decrease in risk. For example, during the Great Recession in the late 2000s, driven by the desire to eliminate risk at any price, investors stampeded into government bonds, ignoring historically low prices for well-regarded companies that were likely to continue to grow over the long term.

The notion of a guarantee appeals to our normal, Reactive desire for security. But if we do not pause and reflect on *who* is making the guarantee and *what* is being guaranteed, then we are very likely to spill.

For example, a bank may promise a certain rate of return on a savings account. While not absolutely certain, the probability that the bank will return the money, with interest, is high. Backing by the FDIC makes that probability even higher. However, the guarantee does not include buying power *if the rate of inflation is higher than the interest rate.* Worse still, someone depositing money in a savings account would forfeit a much greater amount. (On page 35, we contrasted the alarming difference between the return from a savings account at 3% interest and a low-cost, index fund with an average, likely long-term growth rate of 10%. For a weekly $120 contribution over 35 years, the difference would likely be over $1.6 million.)

In other words, the *feeling* connected to the concept of a guarantee can easily lead people to the forfeiture of wealth. In contrast, a tolerance for short-term volatility, and a measured awareness of long-term probabilities, will likely result in far greater wealth. However, in spite of this logic, humans look for certainty (the promise of less risk and effort) in lieu of situations that require significant thought and planning.

The craving for certainty, besides being unrealistic, distracts from the need to weigh probabilities of loss against the likelihood of actual, long-term benefits. As discussed later in the book, the probability of bad outcomes tends to diminish over time and in the right circumstances. But without conscious effort people are tempted to view a lack of certainty as unacceptable risk.

Becoming a "Probabilist"

In the early years of commercial aviation, most people considered air travel too risky. Airplanes were new, unfamiliar technology. To many,
heavier-than-air flying machines seemed to defy reason. They relied on principles of propulsion and lift that were unknown and mysterious to the layman. Spectacular crashes—more common in the early days than now—reinforced people's gut feeling 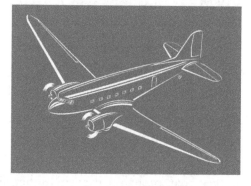 that the convenience of flying was not worth the chance of death or injury. For decades, airlines and plane manufacturers fought against a "headwind" of bias.

Today, apart from those suffering from a clinical fear of flying, this bias has largely vanished. Air travel is considered normal and essential. While the *possibility* of death in an airplane accident is greater than zero, the *probability* is very small. The perception of risk changed and, despite a media preoccupation with crashes, people assume that risk almost without question.

What happened? In the 100-plus years period since the Wright Brothers successfully tested their invention, people have collectively looked at the diminishing probability of bad outcomes and the increasing probability of benefits—convenience and greater mobility. By weighing likely benefits against unlikely bad outcomes, they have largely decided the risk is worthwhile. They have become "probabilists."

Behind this word is a reality that risk-averse investors should take to heart. Being a probabilist is not at all the same as being a fatalist. It simply means that in the absence of certainty, probability is the best criteria for decisions. For decisions involving financial investment, it means that when probable outcomes are internalized and weighed alongside tangible benefits, actions that once seemed risky can become part of normal, everyday life.

When faced with unfamiliar or unknown consequences, it is not wise to let your Reactive biases control your response. Inevitable price fluctuations of investments—especially over the short term—create anxiety in those who are not familiar with long-term trends. However, instead of seeing this environment as too risky, a better course is to weigh the long-term probabilities and benefits. As with air travel, people need to ask, "What is the risk I need to take in order to achieve the likely benefits?" and "How do I minimize the consequences, however small they may be in the long term?"

The first step in becoming a probabalist is to not let others determine the value of an investment. The significance of one's spending is not dictated by its price, which can rise or fall, but by its ability to meet both current and future needs—as discussed in Chapter 5. Once the intrinsic value of an investment is known, the only variable is the probability of failure. If that is sufficiently low—which is often the case—then a Reflective, System 2-using investor will have little trouble in making decisions.

Challenges Ahead

Merely knowing that *feared* risk and *actual* risk are worlds apart does not automatically turn off the Reactive, System 1 "switch." People need to deal with their fear of risk in investment situations in the same way they do with other risks—driving, showering, eating in a restaurant, and flying. They need to:

Become well acquainted with actual probabilities.

Take reasonable steps to minimize bad outcomes.

Understand the potential, long-term benefits.

The last four chapters in this book are designed to help in practical ways with each of these steps when it comes to the type of spending known as investment. But there are also some general attitude adjustments that will help you cope with the feeling of risk:

Always take the full view. Whenever you hear about a price fluctuation—or see one in a graph—ask the question, "What are the missing data?" If the time interval is only a day or a week, demand to see what the trend has been for the past five years. Better still, find out what it has been for the past fifty. If the price change is shown as a "close-up," then pull back to see the bigger picture. A 10-point drop looks significant if all you see is a 20-point range. But if the range is zero to a thousand, 10 points is almost meaningless.

Follow the thinkers, not the storytellers. In every area where people knowingly and calmly take risks, confidence is based on known predictability, not on exceptional stories. Most people fly with an underlying confidence that plane manufacturing and air traffic control are based on well-founded, reliable science—not on personal anecdotes or hunches. The same is true when choosing to invest.

A broadly-based index fund, including only the top companies by market capitalization, is a far better foundation for investment than apocryphal stories of your best friend's uncle who bought Microsoft at $21 a share.

Turn off the noise. Delete or disable the apps and alerts that announce every price shift. Whether someone is considering investment or has already started, looking at prices on a weekly, daily, or hourly basis is a sure recipe for Reactive panic (or overconfidence). Most savvy investment advisors recommend reviews on a monthly or quarterly basis—with good reason. Subjecting oneself to the noise of short-term fluctuations drowns out the overall signal and makes it less likely one would have a Reflective response.

Play like a coach, not like a fan. The vicarious experience of a sports fan is powerful and enjoyable, but it is exactly the wrong model for playing the sport well, or for coaching others to do so. Even if a fan were physically and mentally capable (most aren't), mere excitement and passion cannot replace the practiced skill of an athlete or coach. Similarly, amateur investors may experience the thrill of rising and falling prices—and think themselves able to win more than they lose. In fact, they almost never do. Excitement and passion in the short term does not equip someone to see—and benefit from—the bigger picture.

Lost Yardage Does Not Lose the Game!

In American football, teams suffer frequent setbacks in reaching their primary objective: a successful journey of 100

or fewer yards to the end zone. A failed play can put the ball well back from the starting point, and well short of the short- and long-range goals of the team.

When this happens, the game is not over. To be sure, if there are too many failed plays, the likelihood of a loss is greater. But the mere fact that a quarterback was sacked, or a runner was tackled behind the line of scrimmage, does not mean the game is lost. In fact, such setbacks often inspire teams to new strategies and better play.

The analogy to investments is obvious. A drop in the price of a stock or an index fund does not determine the possible—or even the probable—outcome. If a company's health or per-formance results in consistent, long-term losses which jeop-ardize its long-term success, then index funds like the S&P 500 do what any good coach does in a football game: remove the underperforming player based on a rational, professional decision process.

What short-term losses should not do is create the illusion of unacceptable risk. A momentary loss, seen in context, does not determine the final outcome.

Find a reliable buffer. Speaking of coaches, a good financial advisor can be a valuable defense against the impulse to act Reactively. If they are a bona fide fiduciary (namely, someone legally obligated to act in your best financial interests), a good financial advisor can be the calm voice you need, providing long-term context, perspective, and experience. A good coach will help you overcome your own worst enemy (yourself), resist the urge to panic, and develop a stronger, calmer approach to investing.

The Unseen Risk of Doing Nothing

The fear of performing an unfamiliar action is natural, and the probability of making mistakes initially is high. That is why insurance rates are higher for student pilots than it is for qualified airline pilots. However, once the action is mastered, the anxiety decreases—as does the likelihood of mishaps. The risk, while never zero, falls to a level where we feel confident in doing an activity as a matter of routine. As with driving a car, aversion to making investment choices can be dealt with.

The real risk stems from failing to take a risk at all. Although people experience greater regret for things done badly than for good things neglected, the probability of bad outcomes is much greater for the latter. As shown in subsequent chapters, the consequence of failing to spend on things that appreciate in value will jeopardize our future ability to meet our needs—and the needs of others.

Asking Questions

Before moving on to Chapter 8—on investor versus investment behavior—ask yourself the following question:

What everyday actions do I perform that involve some risk—however small?

In Chapter 10, there are other questions about risk designed to help you pause, reflect, and engage your Reflective, System 2 faculties on this subject.

"Why do so many people buy and sell at the wrong time instead of just staying invested and making a lot more?"

Chapter 8

Investment Behavior vs. Investor Behavior

*"The Stock Market is designed to transfer money
from the Active to the Patient."*
— Warren Buffett

In the previous chapters, we described the "big picture" aspects of what normal behavior is, what it has to do with spending (and spilling) money, and its effect on our perception of wealth and risk. In this chapter, we'll focus on the primary *means* of spending your way to wealth—investment.

Ownership of a successful company is a good example—perhaps the best example—of an asset that increases in value. Unlike electricity, food, vacations, or cars (all valid things on which to spend money), investment in a successful company gives you the probability that, when you sell it, you'll have sufficient financial wealth in the future.

Since most of us cannot afford to own a whole company, we can instead own a piece of it. Each piece is known as a share of stock. This chapter will cover how shares of stock are bought and sold—preferably for multiple companies. More importantly, it will show how and why our normal, *Reactive* (System 1) impulses can make individual *investor behavior* less rewarding than if the individual had applied *Reflective* (System 2) reasoning and let overall *investment behavior* control the results.

Before diving into a discussion of how and why this happens—and how to avoid it—it is important to understand some basic investment terminologies and tools, such as *market index, market capitalization,* and *index funds.*

Tools of the Trade

Despite frequent, short-term declines, the average growth of the general economy has been positive over time. Individual companies have failed on occasion, but other companies grow. They find new ways to meet human needs, develop and sell the resulting products and services to a growing population, and invent ways of doing so more efficiently than their competitors. As long as humans have needs, those who know how to meet those needs will prosper.

This growth potential does not mean success for everyone. Companies that fail to provide a needed product or service, or are inefficient in doing so, will eventually be forced to leave the field. But if the need exists, companies meeting that need will continue to increase in value. Collectively, those that remain in business will continue to expand over the long term.

To the average, normal person, the reasons for an individual company's success or failure at any given moment are hard to fathom—and even harder to predict. To find a useful pattern, the common practice is to view companies collectively. To achieve this, companies are grouped according to an agreed-upon measurement, and the collective results tracked over time. Such a grouping—known as a *market index*—will fluctuate over time, but not as unpredictably as an individual company.

There are different ways to create a market index. Some include companies in the same sector, such as industrial manufacturing or transportation. Some are included on the basis of their price or their dividend earnings. And others are based on market capitalization or *"market cap."* This term simply refers to a company's relative size, using a simple formula:

MARKET CAPITALIZATION =
SHARE PRICE x TOTAL NO. OF OUTSTANDING SHARES

The word "outstanding" simply means the shares that have been authorized by the company, issued (as detailed in the next chapter), and purchased by investors.

So, a hypothetical company with a share price of $100 for each of its 5 billion outstanding shares would have a market capitalization of $500 billion. Market cap is not a predictor of future success or failure. It's simply a way to show the public's opinion of a company's net worth. In this hypothetical example, it simply indicates the fact that it's a big company, according to investors. As of this writing, it would be placed in the top ten.

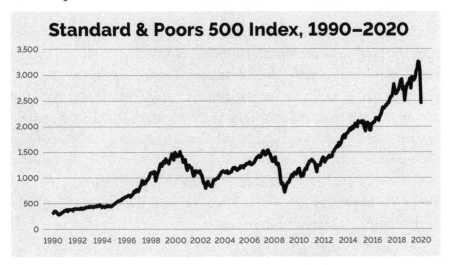

Source: S&P 500 Historical Data, Yahoo Finance

One market index that uses market cap as its criterion for inclusion is the Standard & Poors 500 (the S&P 500). Founded in 1957, it is simply a collection of the 500 major, publicly-traded companies, according to their market capitalization. If an included company's market cap falls below its inclusion criteria, it is replaced by another company, after deliberation by the index's operator.

The S&P 500 market index makes it possible to observe the long-term growth trend of the market—without the need to understand *why*.

There are poor performers within the S&P 500. There have also been short-term reverses, notably during the dot-com bust of 2000–2001 and the financial crisis of 2008–2009. However, over time, the index has increased at an average annual rate of about 10%.

The reason for this is simple. Companies that successfully meet the needs of a growing population will themselves grow. Although nothing is absolutely guaranteed, the likelihood that the 500 largest companies will all suddenly fail is exceedingly small. A much greater probability is that they will collectively succeed and grow. The failure of a few companies—which happens regularly—or even the occasional downturns, does not undo the probability of growth of the indexes.

Market indexes are a convenient way to observe actual financial growth—and to be reasonably confident that such growth will continue. However, to actually take advantage of that growth, the essential practical step is to invest regularly in an *index fund*. This is typically a mutual fund that includes only the companies listed in a specific market index. Besides making regular contributions to an index fund, the investor must also resist the urge to tinker with it. If an investor can do both—make regular contributions and leave them alone—it is extremely likely that one's wealth will grow at the same average rate as that of the 500 largest companies.

Index Fund Basics

In 1974, the late John Bogle founded The Vanguard Group, one of the world's largest investment management companies today. His innovation: a mutual fund whose primary rule was to invest in stocks solely on the basis of their inclusion in the S&P 500 market index. The fund charged clients extremely low fees because the management requirements were simple. Rather than basing decisions on day-to-day analysis of individual stocks, the choice was simply to invest in the 500 largest companies.

The fund, now known as the Vanguard 500 Index Fund, was at first derided by others in the financial industry. However, because its performance was tied to the growth of a market index (in this case the S&P 500), it demonstrated a consistent average growth rate of 10% and soon inspired many imitators.

However, not all index funds are the same. Some charge only a miniscule (.015%) service fee, but some financial firms may charge as much as 1% or more to hold an S&P 500 index fund in the account. Additionally, some firms offer expert management advice—at a price. However, giving investors the option to tinker misses the whole point of investing in an index fund over the long term. The point is to achieve the same, average return as the S&P 500 market index, not to second guess it—which would likely produce a below average return.

Index funds are not the only form of good Investorship spending. Other types of asset allocation will be discussed later in the book. However, for many, a low-cost index fund should comprise a significant portion of one's portfolio. The process for doing so is detailed in Appendix A.

The Trouble with Investor Behavior

With the information available about index funds and their predictably appreciating nature over the long term, a Reflective process should lead most people to buy them and hold onto them until after retirement. It's only logical. However, thanks to our normal, Reactive habits, many individual investors act differently—hoping for above-average results. They tend to be reactive, buying and selling in response to short-term price changes. In almost all cases, this behavior results in poor investment performance.

Above Average?

There are many reasons why people refuse to be satisfied with average, long-term growth in the market *(investment behavior)* and instead attempt to do better in the short term *(investor behavior)*. Many of these reasons are a result of our normal, human tendencies. Consider the following:

In a roomful of normal human beings, when asked for an opinion of their driving ability, a clear majority will say they are above average. This uniquely human response occurs even when those surveyed scored below par in driving hazard perception. Most people also overestimate their own IQ, their powers of persuasion, their generosity, and many other positive traits. Moreover, people believe that facts and circumstances guide *other* people's actions, but *their* personal intentions and desires guide their own actions.

In activities where actual performance levels have no immediate or apparent consequences, people also tend to imagine themselves more capable than they actually are. Those who watch a baseball game may imagine themselves on the field, even though a single inning in a real game would reveal them as below average players. But they are comfortable with the illusion because their daydreaming carries no consequences.

Of course, when considering any group of people, the notion that a majority is above average is mathematically impossible. However, the *feeling* of being above average is normal. It's an unconscious bias known as *illusory superiority*—a phenomenon so pervasive that psychologists take great pains to account for it when studying behavior. People confidently but subjectively believe in their own opinions, predictions, and points of view even when such confidence is not warranted. Some even reject or ignore evidence that reveals the contrary.

As a psychological defense mechanism, the illusion of superiority can be a good thing—a protection of one's self-esteem and sense of self-confidence. However, it can easily become a source of *cognitive errors* and *emotional responses* with long-term, negative results. In areas where the consequences are vague or misunderstood, it is simply easier to believe in one's capabilities than to make a reasoned evaluation. It is difficult to think of oneself as "merely" average. Normal people are tempted to prove—to themselves and others—that they are above average. When it comes to investments, this impulse is nearly always wrong.

"Where All the Children Are Above Average" (Garrison Keillor)

Alexandra Roberts, 35, is an intelligent, capable marketing director for a major software developer. Her generous compensation package includes a retirement account—with options to buy and sell securities within the plan. As a tech-savvy individual, she also has access to detailed information about companies, their histories, and reams of expert analysis, news, and forecasts. Her mobile devices, like those of her peers, provide a constant stream of financially-relevant data.

Two or three times a month, Alex checks the status of her account, noting the price changes of funds and individual stocks within the plan. On occasion, she chats with co-workers about how the plan is doing.

Five years into the plan, Alex recounted her activity. "Naturally, I sold the fund when it seemed the appropriate time to do so," she said, "but I bought it right back as soon as all the concerns had gone away. I only did this occasionally, and each time it was when everybody I knew or listened to or read was doing the same thing. I thought about how volatile the market was. Staying invested just seemed too risky."

Like many of her peers, she sold stocks when the price had gone up (treating them as a "win"), bought new stocks that seemed to have potential, and tended to hold on to stocks whose price had fallen—hoping they would bounce back. *However, as a result of this tinkering, the long-term growth of her investment account averaged only 5% per year!*

This behavior has consequences. Assume that the plan's annual contribution amount was $5,000. At an average growth rate of 5%, the fund would be worth about $29,200 in five years and about $675,000 in 35 years. However, had she allocated the same amount to a low-cost, no-commission S&P index fund with an annual average growth rate of 10%, the results would be far different. If left alone, the index fund would be worth about $32,200 in five years and about $1.8 million in 35 years, before inflation and including dividends.

The five-year difference of "only" $3,000 may seem like a small matter. After all, Alex and her peers are above average in intelligence, believing that their decisions will produce above average results the next time. However, unless they are among the top 1% of those with extraordinary analytical skills, spilling will continue, and the average growth rate will remain at about 5%.

Over a 35-year period, Alex's buying and selling, based on short-term, Reactive thinking, will result in significant spilling. Compared to the predictable investment behavior, her investor behavior will likely result in a forfeiture of *over $1.1 million!*

In the world of investing, "average" is hard to beat. According to UC Berkeley Professor Terrance Odean, individual investor behavior is seldom ideal. Instead of holding well-diversified portfolios and trading only infrequently, they tend to do the opposite. Typical investors trade frequently—selling "winners" and holding "losers"—and hold a poorly diversified portfolio. Many are also unduly influenced by the media and by their own past experience.

Odean's research in behavioral finance reveals that when investors behave this way, their investments consistently perform at a lower rate than the market in general. His study, *Trading Is Hazardous to Your Wealth*, analyzed the trading of over 66,000 households. Those who traded the most earned an average annual return that was 6.5% *less* than the average market return. Other studies found that individual investor trading resulted in systematic and economically large losses—between 2% and 3.8% annually. Odean also noted that only a tiny fraction of frequent traders—1% or less—were able to observe an increase in their account's value, after costs, through their skill in buying and selling stocks.

Investor behavior is also driven by fear of short-term volatility—the narrow notion of risk discussed in Chapter 7. But the opposite can also happen. People make counterproductive moves because of the illusion of superiority and their confidence, however unfounded, that success is more likely in oneself and failure more likely in others.

The Possibility and Certainty Effects
(Emotions Versus Statistics)

The gambling casino industry is built on a mastery of two fields: mathematical probability and behavioral psychology. With absolute precision, casino owners know the mathematical odds of any outcome of any game. They also have a sophisticated knowledge of normal, human behavior. Every game, whether based on cards, dice, wheels, or computerized slot machines, utilizes known, predictable behavior patterns to retain a gambler's interest and maximize his or her losses. (The classic example involves slot machines, which are programmed to give out occasional small wins—or near misses—to motivate the gambler to place bigger bets.)

Investing is *not* the equivalent of casino gambling but there is a common element. Both are subject to the normal, human tendency to subjectively weigh outcomes differently than the facts actually justify.

For example, the Reactive, System 1 bias known as the *possibility effect* makes people likely to assign a high emotional value to events that in fact have a very low probability. Lottery tickets are statistically unlikely to result in a big win but the thrill of *possibly* winning is highly motivating. Likewise, low-probability negative results create a disproportionate sense of fear.

The *possibility* of a big loss, however remote, can motivate undue caution. For example, it can drive an investor to move too large a percentage of his or her portfolio into "safe" instruments like treasury notes or bonds. (See Appendix D.)

Another such bias, *the certainty effect*, causes people to accept a less favorable outcome over a better outcome that is less certain—out of a fear of disappointment. A certain outcome (however improbable in the real world) is given greater emotional weight than a probable one.

The likelihood of success in the investment world is far greater than the emotionally- and statistically-rigged realm of casino gambling. However, the same emotional pitfalls can hinder that success. By recognizing those "situation normal" pitfalls, and by pausing to consider the actual, long-term probabilities, investors can succeed on a consistent basis.

Message System Full; Try Again Later
(Processing Information)

A wife asked her husband to go to the store for a pint of vanilla ice cream and some chocolate syrup. "Do you want me to write that down?" she asked. He replied, "Not a problem; it's only two things." Later he returned with a package of cheddar cheese. "I knew I should have written it down," she said, "and besides, you forgot the crackers."

Humans are limited in their ability to process large amounts of information simultaneously. In studies, researchers have found that most people can only retain four things at a time, and that the brain cannot effectively handle more than two complex, related activities at the same time. The feeling of being able to multitask is an illusion. At best, the human mind can switch rapidly between tasks—but usually at a cost to one's focus and quality of results.

Financial decisions such as evaluating the true value of a company, whether or not to buy or sell it, and being aware of its long-term prospects involves multiple, complex, related activities—far more than most humans can handle. So, we must rely on mental shortcuts to make such decisions. However, this normal, Reactive survival mechanism—one that works well for everyday activities like driving or playing a familiar game—will typically have poor results when it comes to long-term financial strategy. Here are some hazardous mental shortcuts often found in the financial world:

The "instant snapshot" of a market index or stock, often depicted as an over-simplified graphic. The immediate availability of today's price, whether it's up or down, and by how much, triggers an unconscious response. Lacking the time or the patience to consider the larger picture, people tend to use that emotional cue as the basis of buy-or-sell decisions that seem right but are probably not in their long-term interests.

Narrow framing. By looking only at short-term losses or hoped-for gains, without considering the context of the entire portfolio over time, an investor will likely make decisions that result in substantial spilling.

Mental accounting or "keeping score." This is attending to the *emotional value* rather than the actual, well-considered *financial value* in a given transaction. This typically happens in transaction by transaction, stock by stock, without considering the portfolio as a whole. When we limit our perceptions to "winners" and "losers," we are more likely to miss the larger picture and make self-defeating choices.

The herding tendency. Most people are susceptible to the opinions of others, especially when they are perceived as experts. In the financial realm, this herding impulse is magnified by the media. And, since the nuances of spending and wealth are complex and unfamiliar, the urge to follow is overwhelming. Unfortunately, the leader of a particular financial stampede may be subject to the same biases and cognitive errors as everyone else. Unless they have shown a consistent grasp of long-term market regularities, so-called experts can simply overlook what they do not know.

Making Things Worse: Day Trading

The lure of day trading appeals to some more than others. Day trading's reputation has declined over the years, and it is limited to those who have—or think they have—a reserve of money to gamble with. However, a less obvious form of the practice has emerged over the years: the increased ability to "tinker" with traditional investments such as 401(k) retirement accounts.

Originally, retirement accounts had limited options. Employees could select from a number of pre-approved mutual funds or annuities, company stock, or from guaranteed accounts like treasury bonds. However, in response to demand for more flexibility, plans began to add additional fund options, and even allow employees to buy and sell securities within their plan—a practice known as a self-directed brokerage account or SDBA.

On the surface, this seems like a golden opportunity for individuals to "beat the averages" and improve their lot. They can also trade without tax consequences, since all the potential gains (and losses) occur in a retirement account. However, this trend only transplants the perils of day trading to a different, seemingly safe environment. Those who regularly exercise their trading ability within an SDBA are subject to the same cognitive errors as anyone else, and are just as likely to underperform, compared with the market average, and suffer real loss.

Individual investor behavior, even when it is relatively well-informed, nearly always results in a spilling of future wealth. Our increased access to information—amplified by online mobile technology—actually makes the problem worse. With so many choices and options, the Reactive brain looks for cognitive shortcuts rather than use our

Reflective ability to pause, reflect, and consider the likelihood of long-term success with a market index like the S&P 500.

How to Succeed: Investment Behavior

It is perfectly natural to want the best possible result for any human activity. The "pursuit of happiness" ethos inherently motivates people to strive for more than the status quo, and to be unsatisfied with being "merely" average. To do less seems at odds with the sense of self-worth and confidence that are considered virtues.

How, then, in the complex realm of investing, can people be satisfied with the notion that striving to achieve more, while technically possible is statistically improbable? How can they embrace the counterintuitive idea that "average" is actually good?

The psychological reasons for making ill-advised, short-term financial decisions are well established and firmly entrenched in our normal, Reactive biases. Training ourselves to pause and reflect is a challenge—but not an impossible one. Just as people learned to drive—and make driving a matter of habit—they can also incorporate the ideals of Investorship into their everyday spending behavior.

The first beneficial mental shortcut to develop—with plenty of practice and reinforcement—is the belief that "average" is actually quite impressive. An investment spend of *$100 per week* in a no-commission, low-fee, S&P 500 index fund will be worth *over $1.8 million*, before inflation, in only 35 years. Making a habit of such calculations, coupled with looking at short-term price fluctuations less often, will make the Investorship mentality a *normal plus* state of mind.

There are also benefits to *not trying* to game the system and beat the odds. Besides the extreme likelihood of long-term success, taking one's hands off the controls eliminates the anxiety of always trying to do better—giving you more time to enjoy the experience of living.

Investorship habits (motivation, knowledge and understanding, skills, wisdom, and discipline) reduce the risk associated with the law of small numbers in favor of the more desirable and lower risks associated with large numbers—500 companies versus far fewer. They will also eliminate family quarrels over what to do next, help remove many of the human elements that hinder greater achievement and, perhaps most important, foster the high probability of greater success.

Asking Questions

Before moving on to Chapter 9—on the need to create future wealth—ask yourself the following question on the subject of investor behavior versus investment behavior:

What is your first thought or feeling when you see a double-digit or triple-digit change in a stock market index? (Answer the question whether you own stock or not.)

In Chapter 10, there are other questions about risk designed to help you pause, reflect, and engage your Reflective, System 2 faculties on this subject.

*Dad always said, "If you don't change
your ways, you'll end up on the street."*

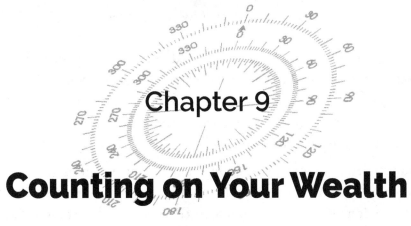

Chapter 9

Counting on Your Wealth

"Twenty years from now you will be more disappointed by the things that you didn't do than by the ones you did do."
—Mark Twain

As we explored in Chapter 6, wealth does not mean being conspicuously rich. It simply means having sufficient monetary wealth to meet basic human needs and the ability to experience non-monetary wealth, such as positive experiences and relationships. Both our monetary and non-monetary wealth stem from our ability to earn—which exists as long as we are able to work.

However, whether you work in a factory, an office, or on the road—doing something mundane or something you love—at some point in time you will have to stop. When that day comes, you will no longer have a source of labor-derived wealth.

"Stop Work Day" is different for everyone. But at some point, your ability to be gainfully employed—and someone else's ability or willingness to give you something of value in return—will no longer exist. When that happens, your actual needs and wants will still be there. In fact, they are very likely to increase. But if you do not have sufficient monetary wealth to meet those needs, you will face a miserable existence.

Just Normal vs. Normal PLUS

Failing to plan for Stop Work Day is all too common. In a recent survey by Bankrate.com, 21% of respondents said that they set aside *nothing* for retirement, emergencies, and other financial needs. In the same survey, 20% said they set aside 5 percent or less, while 28% said they set aside between six and ten percent. Relatively few people set aside the minimum amount needed to meet their necessary financial needs after the paychecks stop.

Our tendency to avoid this reality means that we are normal. Our *Reactive* (System 1) impulses tend to favor gut feelings over statistical information, which requires our focused, *Reflective* (System 2) abilities. We construct coherent, plausible stories out of scraps of data. When confronted with a perplexing question—namely what to do about our future financial security—we tend to make life easier for ourselves by answering a simpler question instead. Rather than ask, "What does this spending decision mean for me in 30 years?" we ask, "How does this spending make me feel?" Even those of us who worry about the future are surprisingly adept at making routine money-spilling spending decisions without anxiety.

Most of all, if we have spent much of our lives *not* spending our financial wealth in ways that will meet our future needs, it is perfectly normal to continue avoiding the subject. Our fear of appearing foolish is a normal, powerful feeling—one that can prevent changes in spending behavior.

The difficulty is that normal behavior can be (and often is) problematic, as we discovered in Chapter 2. When it comes to financial spending and spilling, our intuitive, automatic responses—however normal—will likely result in an inability to adequately meet our needs after Stop Work Day. So, just as we shifted from Reactive to Reflective thinking when we learned to drive or navigate a roundabout, so too, we need to change our spending habits.

At first, this will seem counterintuitive. Rather than spending everything on meeting present needs and wants, we must begin to allocate some of our spending on things that will likely increase in value, despite their momentary price fluctuations. This may mean forgoing an immediate need or want. It is not merely a matter of willpower. It requires some deliberate, Reflective steps:

A Prescription: Planning Ahead for Wealth Accumulation

1. *Find a no-commission S&P 500 index fund* (see Appendix A) and open an account if you don't already have one.

2. *Set up a monthly or weekly process* of making an automatic contribution to the index fund account. (This involves an automatic payment or transfer from a bank checking account—like an automatic mortgage payment, tax withholding, etc.) This process is also covered in Appendix A.

3. *Train yourself not to look at the current price* of your index fund. No matter how easy it may be—through the investment firm's app or website or through daily news reports on the S&P index itself—resist the temptation to check it daily, weekly, or even monthly. Remember that the price today is what someone else is willing to pay today, not a reliable indicator of its long-term value.

4. When you do look at your account—preferably no more than a few times a year—focus on the total contributions to date, since this total will only increase over time and will help you monitor the account's increased value.

5. *Resist the urge to sell* any portion of your "future financial worth" account. This is the act of "tying yourself to the mast," as it were, to prevent you from succumbing to the allure of changing prices and short-term spending needs. Of course, sometimes there may be an urgent, legitimate need for the money. But selling off all or portions of your "future value account" should always be the last resort.

Each of these steps requires the intentional use of slow, deliberate, Reflective thinking. You must resist the normal urge to procrastinate on Steps 1 and 2. And you must especially cultivate the ability to shrug off the constant noise about price and short-term volatility—distractions that tempt you to deviate from Steps 3, 4, and 5.

This is admittedly a difficult task—just as learning to drive once was. However, once these habits are established and reinforced by evidence of financial growth over time, they will become a successful part of your routine. Instead of being just *normal* (a recipe for misery), you will become *normal plus*. Your spending routine will include less financial spilling and more long-term spending on things that increase in value.

The Moment of Decision

The shift from Reactive to Reflective thinking involves a relatively simple equation: *What price are we willing to pay for the ability to meet our needs and wants in the future?* The ability to do so has intrinsic value. Maintaining one's physical existence—plus a reasonable amount of non-monetary wealth—is unquestionably a good thing. And even though we don't know how long we'll be around, it's certainly essential to have a sufficient amount of monetary wealth when you arrive at Stop Work Day.

Barring some unlikely windfall, the price for having sufficient monetary wealth at that point involves investing in things that will increase in value. For some, real estate is one such asset. However, although real estate generally appreciates in value, it is not easy to convert into spendable wealth, and is very difficult to dispose of in small segments or increments. Other assets contained in pension funds, 401(k) plans, IRAs, and the like—even if they manage to overcome inflation (as many do not)—are seldom sufficient to meet the owner's financial needs over long periods of time. For this reason, it is almost always necessary to have additional funds designated for future financial needs.

It is therefore essential to have a sufficient portion of your future financial wealth invested in assets that can be converted into spendable cash, as needed—*after* Stop Work Day. Until then, however, you should never "raid" or "tinker" with such accounts. As discussed in

Chapter 8, the temptation to buy and sell within an investment account almost always results in less value than if it was left alone.

The most reliable means of assuring adequate future monetary wealth is surprisingly simple. If a certain amount of money is regularly spent on assets that are likely to increase in value over the long term—such as a low-cost S&P index fund—then a multiplier effect occurs. (See Appendix B.) Depending on the amount of money invested, the time allowed, and the *average* rate of return, the likelihood of having ample monetary wealth after Stop Work Day is extremely high.

Timing Is Important

Although the path to such monetary wealth is clear, it is not the same for everyone. If you start investing regularly at a young age, then smaller amounts will result in the probability of a sufficient level of monetary wealth over time. If you start later, then more must be spent to achieve comparable results. To see what this means, use the Investorship calculator provided with this book (www.investorship.com/calculator). For example, a monthly contribution of $300 in a no-commission S&P 500 index fund with an *average*, long-term growth rate of 10% will have significantly different results for a 25-year-old than for someone aged 55:

Starting Age	RESULTS OF **$300 MONTHLY** CONTRIBUTION BY AGE: (based on S&P 500 index fund calculations, including dividends)				
	35	45	55	65	75
25	$64,276	$253,099	$772,567	**$2,159,856**	**$5,811,785**
35	$0	$64,276	$253,099	$772,567	$2,159,856
45		$0	$64,276	$253,099	$772,567
55			$0	**$64,276**	**$253,099**
65				$0	$64,276

(Figures not adjusted for inflation.)

Although there is a vast difference between these figures, all is not lost for those entering the process late. By increasing the amount contributed, the same multiplier will produce better results. Assuming that someone 45 and older is able to contribute $300 *per week*, the model changes significantly:

Starting Age	RESULTS OF **$300 WEEKLY** CONTRIBUTION BY AGE: (based on S&P 500 index fund calculations, including dividends)				
	45	55	65	75	85
45	$0	$278,532	$1,096,766	$3,347,791	$9,359,379
55		$0	**$278,532**	**$1,096,766**	**$3,347,791**
65			$0	$278,532	$1,096,766

(Figures not adjusted for inflation.)

Clearly, if one's investing process starts later, it's more likely that Stop Work Day will have to be postponed—if possible. However, the formula itself is clear, and provides a solid basis for making good Investorship decisions. The earlier one decides to regularly allocate spending on things that significantly increase in value, the more financial wealth one will have to meet one's future needs.

The Marshmallow Factor and the Lightbulb Moment

In Chapter 6, we used the well-known "marshmallow experiment" to illustrate how hard it is to defer gratification when faced with an immediate prospect of something desirable. Like the children in the experiment, we naturally find it difficult to resist spending money for an immediate reward. It is hard to wait for a greater future reward— something that feels less gratifying in the present moment.

No matter what age you are, you allocate *all* of your financial wealth. You spend it on things that either decrease or increase in value. Our normal tendency is to do the former and ignore or delay the latter. However, at almost any age, you can change how you allocate your financial wealth by reducing the spending behavior that constitutes spilling and choosing instead to spend differently.

In Jonathan Swift's satire, *Gulliver's Travels*, the miniscule Lilliputians suffered from an absurd level of reactive, short-sighted (pun intended) thinking. Gulliver, a normal-sized human, epitomized the ability to see the world in a larger context. This is a useful analogy when it comes to our approach to spending and wealth. By looking at them more from Gulliver's perspective and less from that of the Lilliputians, we can alter the last part of our story, and have sufficient financial wealth when Stop Work Day arrives.

In Chapter 3, we related three different stories with similar conclusions. In each case, the person unwittingly spilled enormous sums of money by spending what seemed to be trivial amounts. In each case, the loss was not only in the money spent at the time, but also in the forfeiture of greater financial wealth had the spending been on something that would, in all probability, dramatically increase over time.

The people in these stories possess all the normal, cognitive biases and preconceptions that define our species. If and when they become aware of the problem of spilling, they are still normal—and prone to making the same mistakes. Admittedly, it takes time to learn new habits, and to become less reactive and more reflective in the face of the financial news of the day—to become *normal plus*. However, the fact is that normal people *can* change their own behavior.

The Lightbulb Moment

Tania Gilman's unconscious habit of leaving the lights on was one of many seemingly insignificant spending practices. Over a 40-year period, the spending of about $47,000 on lighting unoccupied rooms was actually a forfeiture of over $283,000—had the money been invested in a no-commission, index fund with an average, long-term growth rate of 10%.

Of course, the lightbulb issue was only the beginning. Once Tania and her husband, Jim, added up this and other similar instances of spilling, the lightbulb went off, so to speak. They began listing other ways they were spilling—from buying name brand items (rather than generic ones) to buying lattés (over getting their own espresso machine). They even figured out ways to control lighting with a smartphone. It added up. Their total unnecessary spilling averaged $11.76 per week—which meant a forfeiture of about $366,887 over a 40-year period!

Their "lightbulb moment" led them to act. Despite the natural tendency to procrastinate or view the stock market with suspicion, both Tania and Jim approached their respective employers with a proposal. Using the $11.76 weekly figure as a benchmark, they convinced their benefits managers to contribute that amount into an S&P 500 index fund. Eventually, they also set up their own autopay routines, to make additional regular payments into the fund.

Knowing that the temptation to withdraw funds would often occur, they also took steps to curtail their own ability to easily withdraw from their investment accounts:

- Many investment accounts include the option of checks or a debit card to access funds more easily. Tania and Jim declined that offer.

- If a bank is involved, such accounts can be accessed online and viewed alongside one's regular checking and savings accounts. They chose not to put their investment accounts within easy reach of their day-to-day banking activity.

- Nearly all investment accounts include an online, mobile app. This convenient technology provides instant access to the fund's current price, along with tools for making trades or withdrawing funds. Tania and Jim chose not to install the app in order to eliminate the temptation to make changes.

- Another option for such accounts is to receive regular, electronic statements—along with updates and alerts—via email. They opted for paper-only statements and no emails.

In other words, they chose to "lash themselves to the mast," making it more difficult to succumb to the normal urge to sell when prices declined in the short term.

Tania and Jim also began to establish another important habit. Rather than reviewing their fund's price on a daily or weekly basis, they would look at the numbers only every 3–6 months. The most important number in the report was the total they had contributed—which would always increase. If a genuine financial emergency arose, or they needed to fund an important life event like their children's education, they treated the possibility of selling fund assets as the extreme last resort.

Over time, Tania and Jim learned to shrug more when stock prices changed, and instead focused on other, more important things. Having made a viable plan for their future financial wealth, they were better able to acquire and enjoy more non-financial wealth.

Becoming *normal plus* involves a conscious awareness of all the factors described in this book, including a firm grasp of reactive versus reflective thinking, and the nature of spending, wealth, and risk. It also involves the knowledge that individual investors following their own impulses almost always fare worse than the market as a whole. Above all, it involves an understanding that price and value are generally not the same thing.

With such knowledge, a person can become *normal plus* by taking steps that at first feel counterintuitive but ultimately provide a *satisfaction* that ordinary, normal spending behavior cannot.

In order to avoid the long-term misery that normal, Reactive spending behavior will eventually produce, we have the opportunity to modify that behavior. Resisting the urge to "take the marshmallow" is difficult, especially in this era of instant information. However, once we have that lightbulb moment—the realization that our spending is actually spilling—we have the opportunity to become *normal plus*—able to shrug more, appreciate the difference between price and value, and derive ever greater satisfaction from our long-term spending habits.

In the next chapters, we'll take a look at the path forward. To be less reactive and more reflective when it comes to spending and investment—to become *normal plus*—we need to ask ourselves the right questions. At first, this will not seem natural. However, with practice, asking these questions will help us pause, shrug off the constant barrage of financial news, and attain the calmer, long-term perspective that will ensure our future financial wealth.

Asking Questions

Before moving on to Chapter 10, ask yourself the following question on the subject of planning your future wealth:

Approximately how much monetary wealth will you possess when you no longer receive a paycheck for your labor?

People always wondered why Seymour was so wealthy when he always looked at things so differently.

Chapter 10

Now It's Your Move!

"You miss 100% of the shots you don't take."
— Wayne Gretzky

Throughout this book, we have emphasized the need to do things differently from what normal people do. In matters of spending and investment—indeed, in all of life—we must become what I call *normal plus*. The most important question, then, is "How do I get there?"

When it comes to spending strategy, *normal plus* (Investorship) behavior has two main components. They involve:

Increasing the amount of money allocated to appreciating assets. This may seem obvious, but in reality, it takes practice and patience. Even when you have a "lightbulb moment" (like Tania Gilman's realization in Chapter 3 that leaving lights on represents a potential six-figure wealth forfeiture over 40 years), changing your spending habits is not easy or automatic. The realization that you will require sufficient wealth to meet your needs *after* you stop working has to be accompanied by action. Only by taking deliberate spending steps today—as outlined in Chapter 6—and "lashing yourself to the mast," as it were, will you begin making *normal plus*, Investorship habits a permanent part of your life.

Strengthening your tolerance for asset price volatility and its associated perceived (typically misperceived) risk. The S&P 500 index experiences an *average* change of 25% from its yearly high to its yearly low, which is alarming if you have a short-term outlook and are confused about price and value. Reacting in the moment to this precipitous change, while perfectly normal, almost always results in buying and selling volatile assets at precisely the wrong time. As we discussed in Chapter 8, this is the reason why individual investors' financial returns almost always tend to be lower than the investments themselves (particularly index funds) over the long term.

The Financial Advisor's Role

An important part of becoming *normal plus* may, and often does, involve finding the right advice. It's true that, like us, professional financial advisors can be reactive rather than reflective. They can be subject to the same cognitive errors about spending and wealth as other people. However, this book is by no means an indictment of the profession. There are sound advisors and sound advice to be found—provided the professional you engage has a *fiduciary* responsibility to act in your best interests financially. What is a fiduciary-financial advisor? It is a person or firm that is legally compelled to do *only* what is in your financial best interest. It is not sufficient that they recommend things that are suitable for you. *By law,* they are only permitted to recommend courses of action where your financial interests are paramount.

A principle task of a true fiduciary-financial advisor is to help clients achieve a level of financial wealth that exceeds that of normal investors. To do so, such advisors must have a command of what constitutes long-term value—regardless of short-term price fluctuations. They must be able to increase their clients' tolerance for volatility and correct their clients' misperception that such volatility is not necessarily synonymous with risk. Such tolerance for volatility must rise to the point where clients can maintain a level of appreciable assets that enable them to achieve their targeted financial goals. In addition, a fiduciary-financial advisor must reassure and encourage clients to fund their future wealth accounts with additional money needed to assure attainment of their financial goals.

In short, a good fiduciary-financial advisor can play a major role in helping you avoid the perils of normal, reactive thinking and become *normal plus* when it comes to spending and investing.

Moving from Normal to Normal PLUS

With that in mind, let's review the chapters and ask some practical questions that will help you identify your present beliefs and behavior and steer you toward becoming *normal plus*.

Changing Habits

In Chapter 2, The Problem with Normal, we discussed what it means to be a normal human being:

- We use automatic, **Reactive** (System 1) thinking to pilot through everyday situations efficiently—often without much conscious thought. But this instinct can often lead to poor results.

- System 1 thinking also involves *personal biases*. These biases can sometimes result in cognitive errors, leading us to make decisions with less than ideal outcomes.

- We are often resistant to changing our familiar patterns.

- But change is quite possible if we learn to use **Reflective** (System 2) thinking to address new circumstances. Doing so requires conscious effort, but eventually we can acquire new habits that better serve the need.

QUESTION:

What is an activity I do every day without thinking much about it or remembering the details afterwards? (It's OK to list more than one activity.)

QUESTION:

What is a personal bias or preference I have for one thing over another? How may some personal biases or preferences I hold influence my financial behavior?

QUESTION:

What normal action—even an innocuous one—has recently led me to a result that was different from the one I expected? Did it have a financial consequence?

QUESTION:

When I found myself doing something automatically that had poor results, how did I stop doing that particular thing and start doing otherwise? How can I apply what I learned to my investment habits?

Moving Towards Less Spilling

In Chapter 3, we explained the difference between spending and spilling our wealth:

- Spending is a choice, a decision to give something of value in exchange for something else of value. We spend in order to meet a need or satisfy a want or desire.

- Spending involves more than just money. It also involves time, energy, and effort. It also includes intangible but very real things such as reputation and trust.

- When we fail to weigh the full value—including the future value—of the thing received in exchange for our spending, we tend to spend far more than we need on things that *decrease* in value and less on things that *increase* in value. This results in a forfeiture of enormous future financial wealth—a phenomenon we call *spilling*.

- The results of spilling can be calculated, but because we tend to trust our normal, intuitive feelings about spending, our normal, Reactive biases often lead us to spill more than we should.

- If spilling prevents us from satisfactorily meeting our *future* needs and wants, then we must acquire the habit of pausing, reflecting, and adopting a deliberate strategy to minimize spilling and spend more on things that increase in value.

QUESTION:

In what spending activities am I most inclined to spill? (Use the Spilling Journal on page 39 to figure it out.)

QUESTION:

What can I do to prevent spilling? (From your Spilling Journal, think about the lower-cost alternatives and how they meet your real needs.)

Moving from Shallow Wealth to Deep Reward

As discussed in Chapter 3, wealth and reward are concepts we tend to view positively, but without understanding them fully.

- Financial wealth is ultimately a reward for one's labors and investments, and an assurance that both present and future needs can be met.

- Money is a means of doing this, but money is not the sole component of wealth. Our core values—our store of non-monetary capital—dictate that we broaden our notion of wealth to include intangible, sometime unglamorous goals that meet our own needs as well as those of others.

- A shallow notion of wealth—the possession of highly-visible, status-oriented objects that decline in value—must be replaced by a new spending model that includes a larger proportion of assets that increase in value. These are typically inconspicuous.

- In today's consumer culture, this basic concept seems strange. But in order to spend your way to wealth, you must be able to apply the same practices involved in making fine wine: sound principles, the right ingredients, and time.

QUESTION:

What are three examples of monetary wealth you currently possess?

_____

_____

QUESTION:

What are three examples of NON-monetary wealth you currently possess?

_____

_____

QUESTION:

What amount of monetary wealth would be sufficient to meet your basic needs in the present? (An exact figure is not required.) *Will that amount remain the same in the future?*

- -

- -

QUESTION:

What amount of non-monetary wealth (experiences, relationships, etc.) do you need in order to lead a satisfactory life? How much of this non-monetary wealth requires the expenditure of monetary wealth?

- -

- -

Moving from Fear of Risk to Becoming a Probabilist

In Chapter 7, Demystifying Risk, we discussed the fear of doing something unfamiliar and of making mistakes in the process.

- Apprehension is normal and natural when attempting anything new. The probability of mistakes is also higher, which is why insurance rates are higher for young drivers and student pilots than for experienced drivers and qualified airline pilots.

- However, once the action is mastered, the anxiety decreases—as does the likelihood of mishaps. The risk falls to the level where we feel confident in doing an activity as a matter of routine.

- As flying or driving for the first time is discomforting, so too are our first investing decisions. However, our aversion to making investment choices can also be managed with conscious, Reflective effort. The real risk stems from failing to take a risk at all.

- Although people experience greater regret for things done badly than for good things neglected, the probability of bad outcomes is much greater for the latter. The consequence of failing to spend on things that appreciate in value will jeopardize our future ability to meet our needs—and the needs of others.

QUESTION:

What everyday actions do I perform that involve some risk—however small?

QUESTION:

When I first did something new, and even potentially dangerous, how afraid did I feel? Did those feelings lessen over time?

QUESTION:

Have I ever refused to try something because I feared a bad outcome?

QUESTION:

How did I overcome my fears when I had to try something new or unfamiliar? How can I apply what I learned to my investment behavior?

Moving from Investor Behavior to Investment Behavior

In Chapter 8, Investor Behavior Versus Investment Behavior, we described the negative results of typical investor behavior and the positive outcomes of investment behavior:

- Despite frequent, short-term declines, the average growth of the general economy has been positive over time.

- Individual companies have failed on occasion—as they will continue to do. However, other companies—those that efficiently meet human needs with their products and services—will grow, replacing those that fail to do so. Collectively, such growth will financially benefit the respective business owners (shareholders) over the long term.

- Despite this consistently upward trend, individual investors nearly all buy and sell stocks to their own disadvantage. Individual investor performance, with few exceptions, is lower than the market average. Those who refrain from short-term trading in response to price fluctuations and instead remain invested in appreciable assets over the long term tend to do far better.

- The urge to buy and sell over short periods of time is a normal response, albeit a self-defeating one. Seeing a sudden rise or fall in the price of a stock, or of an index fund, can produce a predictable reaction—one that will almost always be wrong in some way. A reflective, deliberate response, refraining from sudden action, and considering the long-term likelihood of success, is the hallmark of a *normal plus* investor, and will produce far better results.

QUESTION:

What is your first thought or feeling when you see a double-digit or triple-digit change in a stock market index? (Answer the question whether you own stock or not.)

QUESTION:

Assume that you need to fund an important life event and must sell some stock to do so. If you own stock in two companies—one performing well and the other less so—which one would you sell?

QUESTION:

How many sources of information about markets and stock prices do you read, watch, or listen to every day?

QUESTION:

How could you limit or ignore your exposure to daily or hourly market news?

Moving Our Focus from Price to Value

In Chapter 5, we defined and discussed the often-confused terms, *price* and *value*.

- Value is the usefulness or desirability of a product, service, or entity. It can be functional—offering some practical use over a known period of time. It can be social—providing greater status or better connection with others. It can also be psychological—providing personal satisfaction, fond memories, or other emotional benefits. But because individuals and circumstances are so varied, value is difficult to quantify.

- When someone perceives—subjectively—that something has value, then that object or service has worth to that person. This varies widely, but the worth of a product or service to each individual will dictate what he or she is willing to give in exchange for it. Depending on the available supply (and the seller's perception of what it's worth to give it up), the resulting consensus has a dollar figure—the price.

- When it comes to companies—or portions of companies represented by shares of stock—the same principles apply. The price of a stock is what a buyer is willing to pay, and a seller is willing to accept. The value of the company over a short time period is usually relatively stable, but the price of its stock will most likely vary from day to day—or moment to moment—based solely on the perceptions (often misperceptions) of buyers and sellers.

- The long-term change in a company's worth will ultimately affect the price people are willing to pay, but the rapidly changing price is seldom an accurate indicator of its value.

QUESTION:

If you owned a house, valued for tax purposes at $300,000, and had no plans to move, what would you say to a person knocking at your door offering to buy it for $250,000? What if they offered $350,000?

QUESTION:

What price would you be willing to pay for full, legal ownership of one acre of land in a swamp? What questions would you ask before offering that price?

QUESTION:

If you owned an index fund of multiple stocks priced at approximately $20,000, and the price rose or fell by 15% in one week, what would its price likely be in 30 years?

- -

- -

Moving from Instant Gratification to Long-Term Security

In Chapter 7, Counting on Your Wealth, we covered the need for financial security after that inevitable point in time when you will no longer have a source of labor-derived income.

- The timing of "Stop Work Day" is different for every individual. But whenever it happens, your actual needs and wants will still be there. In fact, the costs of satisfying those needs and wants are very likely to have increased.

- If you do not have sufficient monetary wealth to meet the costs of satisfying those needs, you will face a most unfortunate and highly undesirable existence.

- In order to avoid the long-term consequences that normal spending (spilling) behavior will eventually cause, we must seize the opportunity to modify our behavior.

- Once we realize that much of our spending is actually spilling, we have taken the first step in becoming *normal plus*. We will have mastered the art of shrugging off unnecessary and emotion-jarring noise and focus instead on recognizing the difference between price and value. In so doing, we will derive ever greater satisfaction from our long-term spending habits and our ensuing financial wealth.

QUESTION:

What percentage of your current spending is on assets that appreciate in value?

- -

- -

QUESTION:

Approximately how much monetary wealth will you possess when you no longer receive a paycheck for your labor?

- -

- -

QUESTION:

Will that amount be sufficient to meet your needs to your satisfaction?

- -

- -

QUESTION:

What spending activities can you do differently—starting now—to change the amount of monetary wealth you have at Stop Work Day?

- -

- -

Conclusions

This book deals with spending in its broadest possible sense, including the many ways we unconsciously *spill* money. When we spend too much on things that decrease in value and spend too little or nothing on things that increase in value, we forfeit huge potential financial wealth and jeopardize our ability to thrive in the future. We spill when we think only in the immediate present rather than consider the bigger picture—because we are normal.

The purpose of this book has been to inform and enlighten the reader about our normal human behavioral tendencies that prevent us from realizing the benefits of an Investorship spending philosophy. The goal was to inspire the reader to become financially *normal plus*. When executed properly and consistently, this spending philosophy assures the attainment not only of financial wealth but also of all the other important non-financial wealths that make living worthwhile. This includes a wealth of experiences, relationships, and satisfaction beyond mere physical comforts. In other words, by living this spending philosophy, one can achieve a great measure of inner contentment and enduring happiness through an abundance of wealths.

By becoming a *normal plus* individual, you will find yourself in the company of many of our country's most distinguished and successful financial decision makers, including Warren Buffet, Bill Gates, Sam and Alice Walton, and many others. Also, remember that wealth is not always dollar-denominated, as with Mother Teresa (a wealth of compassion and generosity), the Dalai Lama (a wealth of compassion and dedication), and Mahatma Gandhi (a wealth of vision).

Investorship spending will result in satisfaction and happiness—a happiness that extends to all of the important people in our lives. By asking ourselves the right questions and adopting the right mindset and its behavioral steps, we can achieve the goal of spending our way to wealth.

The Final Chapter

Spending can be the cause of wealth.

— or —

Spending can be the cause of wealth forfeiture—and regret.

It's your choice.

Epilogue

The Last Word

Now that you've finished the book—what's next? I've dropped some clues along the way, but this is the perfect time to start putting these concepts into action.

On Page 39 ("My Spilling Journal"), I asked you to estimate the total amount of money you spill each month. You can either track the actual amounts or use a common-sense rule of thumb, such as 5% of your total spending. Whatever the figure, write it down here:

$_____ SPILLED PER MONTH

Then go to the Calculator at www.investorship.com/calculator and type in the above figure, set the frequency to Monthly, press Calculate and write down the results here:

$_____ IN 10 YEARS

$_____ IN 20 YEARS

$_____ IN 30 YEARS

$_____ IN 40 YEARS

$_____ IN 50 YEARS

Now, before you put down the book, be sure to do two more things:

- Open an account with any of the firms that offer low-cost S&P 500 index funds. (Four of them are listed in Appendix A, but there are others. Another option, also described in Appendix A, is the Target Date fund.)

- Opening an account is a simple first step, but you need not start allocating money just yet. Instead, set yourself a reminder on your phone to do so. Your normal response will be to procrastinate on this, so set the reminder for 10 days from now—at a time of day where you'll be able to act.

OK. You can put the book down now—after bookmarking this page. But after you do that, spend some time thinking about what you've read. Some quality reflection time will help you mentally prepare for the next step.

When your reminder sounds, don't ignore it.

Instead, log in to your account and set up an automatic, monthly payment from your regular checking or savings account. For the amount, just use the number written above. You can always increase it later on. Also, be sure to specify that any earnings or dividends from the account be automatically added back to the account itself. Also, some accounts include a separate "cash" account. Be sure to set up an automatic transfer (buy order) from that account to your index fund.

If you follow these steps, you have begun spending your way to wealth. There's little else you need to do! However, some important precautions should be noted here:

- Wherever possible, turn off any electronic status reports or alarms the investment firm may offer. That includes emails, mobile alerts, and the like. Rather than installing the firm's mobile app, let all your account information come to you the old-fashioned way—by mail. As we discussed in Chapter 8 ("Investment Behavior Versus Investor Behavior"), reacting to immediate fluctuations all but guarantees a poorer financial outcome.

- When the automatic payment to your index fund posts, don't panic. What seems like a loss of funds in the short term is actually an enormous probable gain in the long term. If you need some emotional support, enter your monthly contribution amount in the Investorship Calculator (Appendix B) and look at the projected outcome.

- Speaking of the calculator, create a shortcut to it on your mobile device.

- On occasion, perhaps two or three times a year, it is wise to look at your investment account—not for the short-term fluctuations but to track the increasing total. This is usually a good time to consider increasing your monthly contribution.

- It's also a good idea to work with a financial professional who shares your views on long-term financial strategy. If he or she is a true fiduciary, their mandate is to advise according to your long-term interests. Such a professional will also serve to calm your fears and resist the temptation to "do something now."

I trust this book has opened up a new appreciation for how normal you really are and provided a pathway to becoming *normal plus* in matters of spending and wealth. If you can apply the principles of slowing down and reflecting on outcomes rather than reacting to short-term stimulus, then I am confident you will be on your way to greater wealth and satisfaction.

Please feel free to share your experiences with me. I am always encouraged when I see the light bulb moment—and even more encouraged when that leads to long-term success.

Appendix A
The Investorship Checklist

According to Investopedia, index funds are portfolios of stocks or bonds designed to mimic the composition and performance of a financial market index. They are based on the idea that in the long term, the market will outperform any single investment. Index funds do not require much in the way of active, day-to-day management and so have fewer expenses and fees.

Throughout this book, we have discussed the long-term growth potential of S&P 500 index funds. These are professionally managed investment funds that pool money from many investors to purchase stocks from among the approximately 500 major U.S. companies selected by Standard & Poor—a rating services company owned by Moody's Inc. This Appendix will outline the basic steps involved in setting up and using these index funds—if you choose to do so on your own. It will also help you ask the right questions if you work with a professional financial advisor on such matters.

Investing in an S&P index fund diversifies a person's holdings among shares of major American companies. The fund price changes daily as does the S&P Index that it mirrors. As such, the holder of the fund can expect the price to fluctuate by up to 25% from its yearly high to its

The Checklist
- [ ] Select a Fund
- [ ] Open an Account
- [ ] Set Up a Regular, Automatic Contribution
- [ ] "Lash Yourself to the Mast"

yearly low. However, over the past 50+ years, its yearly returns have averaged about 10%, including dividends.

The perceived risk in owning such a fund is stock market volatility in general. This is due to the normal human tendency to react to day-to-day price changes—based on people's *daily* differences of opinion regarding the company's value. Over time, however, these differences of opinion regarding the company's value will be replaced by updated majority opinions of the company's actual value. Despite the inevitable, short-term price fluctuations, major American companies have proven themselves to be sound investments over the long term.

Select a Fund

While many index funds select stocks from companies included in the S&P 500 index, *not all index funds are the same!* Some impose large fees that burden its performance. In theory, however, such excess fees are not necessary since the actual cost to mimic the actual S&P 500 index is minimal. A company's inclusion in the S&P 500 index is not based on complex calculations of potential business value but on the company's size.

The funds shown below are available without commissions and have very low yearly charges of around .01% or about ten cents for every $1000 invested. In alphabetical order, and with no implied endorsement—or implication that they are the only such funds, they are:

- Fidelity 500 Index Fund (FXAIX)
- Schwab S&P 500 Index Fund (SWPPX)
- T. Rowe Price Equity Index 500 Fund (PREIX)
- Vanguard 500 Index Fund Investor Shares (VFINX)

When looking at these index funds—on your own or with assistance—it is important to confirm that there are no commissions, and that the yearly charges are in fact low.

Each company has its own website, of course, but it's easy to be distracted by options and detailed descriptions. By searching for the specific fund's five-letter code, you can more easily get to the right page.

An Alternative

This book extols the virtues of owning an S&P 500 index fund. However, such a fund need not be the only option. An equally simple solution, by itself or in addition to an S&P 500 index fund, is the Target Date fund, advocated by noted financial professionals such as Paul Merriman. Such funds are also comprised of multiple companies and the fund is regularly contributed to over time. However, the mix of companies shifts to become more conservative at a predetermined point in time—usually at retirement. Like an S&P 500 index fund, a Target Date fund does not require regular buying and selling of individual stocks, which usually produces poorer results.

Open an Account

If you don't already have an account at an investment firm offering an S&P 500 index fund and/or a Target Date fund, opening one is usually straightforward—often similar to opening a bank or credit card account. It can be done in person (if the fund's managing company has an office in your area) or over the phone. Of course, it can also be done online.

To ensure your privacy, and because financial services is a highly-regulated industry, the information forms are very detailed, and various identity confirmations will be required. As with other, sensitive financial matters, your online login and password information should be created and recorded with extreme care. If a spouse or significant other is to be named on the account, then they too must submit and verify their information.

While setting up the account, there are several *options* to consider:

6. Most companies offering S&P index funds also offer a vast array of other investment alternatives—none of which are within the scope

of this book's endorsement of an S&P 500 index fund. These other investment alternatives provide the option to initiate stock trades within the account. As we discussed in Chapter 5, the ability to buy and sell individual stocks within an account often result in poorer performance than if the investment had been left alone in an S&P 500 index fund. Therefore, it the book's premise that you are well counseled to decline these options.

7. If an S&P 500 Index fund has a dividend and other income re-invested in share of the same fund, it's usually wise to have these funds automatically deposited back to the fund itself. This should also apply to any contributions you make. Incoming funds of any kind should never go to the equivalent of a checking account; they should automatically go into your actual S&P 500 index fund.

8. Most firms offering S&P 500 Index funds also provide banking services, including checks and even debit cards to allow for easy access to the money. It can be tempting but, since the main tenet of the Investorship philosophy is to spend towards long-term growth, declining those liquidity options is probably best.

9. Most investment firms offer multiple ways of reporting your current account status—from paper statements to email notifications, text messages, and mobile alerts. As we discussed in the book, it is normal and instinctive to read and study each such report thoroughly and carefully. However, one of the key tenets of the Investorship philosophy is to not be distracted or alarmed by excessive levels of noise that tempt us to take sudden action when the wiser course is to pause and reflect. So, in many cases, it is often wiser to "just say no" to electronic communication and stick with occasional (quarterly or yearly) paper reports.

Set Up a Regular, Automatic Contribution

Once an account is established, you can contribute to it whenever you wish, by sending a check or making one-time or periodic transfers into the account. However, as normal human beings, we tend to procrastinate with such tasks—especially it they're new to us. To combat this, it's a good idea to set up a regular, automatic payment to your S&P 500 index fund account.

This is usually a simple step—done one time—within your new account. Under Contributions on the firm's website, you identify your regular bank account (by routing number and account number), specify the amount and day of the month you want the payment to occur, and click "submit." Once your bank has been verified by the fund, contributions will be made automatically, until you change the schedule. This can be an important step in the process of assuring that you spend your way to wealth.

When selecting the amount to contribute, be sure to explore the Investorship Calculator described in Appendix B. By entering an amount and a frequency interval, you'll be able to see what that contribution will likely be worth in the future—5 to 50 years from now. This is an excellent way to remind yourself of the long-term, highly probable wealth buildup that will result from each addition to your S&P 500 index fund. You can always change the amount of the regular contribution—preferably upwards—but for the initial setup it's always encouraging to see the future potential.

There are two warnings when it comes to setting up a regular, automatic contribution:

1. Procrastination is a powerful force. Spending your way to wealth is not customary for most people, so the temptation to put it off will be strong. *Don't give in to that temptation.*

2. When the first few automatic payments occur, the urge to react will be strong. Seeing your bank account balance decline can be disconcerting. But remember: a decrease in your bank accounts balance is offset by a corresponding increase in your fund's holdings. The solution, therefore, is to pause, reflect, and consider the future value of that regular contribution.

"Lash Yourself to the Mast"

In Chapter 4, we used the ancient Greek hero Ulysses as a metaphor for resisting temptation. Not wanting to wreck his ship by heeding the seductive call of the Sirens, Ulysses had his crew members put wax in their ears after they tied him to the mast. Hence, they wouldn't be able to hear the Sirens' song and he himself was incapable of turning the rudder and striking the rocks that would destroy his ship.

When it comes to owning an investment-brokerage account, the temptations to buy and sell reactively are many and frequent. In addition to cable news reports and financial mobile apps, your own S&P 500 index fund account probably comes with a convenient mobile app for your smartphone. In addition to the flood of daily stock market news, the app also gives you the power to log in and view your fund's current price from almost anywhere—at any time. When combined with regular emails and texts, all this financial input collectively amounts to noise. It is a formidable chorus of Sirens, tempting you to act immediately. Recognize that it is unworthy of being called news and refer to it more accurately as noise. Disregard it!

As we've discussed throughout the book, our normal, Reactive habits are often aggravated by this kind of noise—making it difficult to pause, reflect, and generally apply our *normal plus*, Reflective reasoning. So, in addition to limiting our investment status to occasional printed reports (see account options, above) it may also be wise to limit, or even uninstall, the mobile app that came with your account.

This does not mean ignoring your account completely. Being able to see your contributions accumulate and grow is one of the great incentives to continued Investorship philosophy habits. However, instant access to the "breaking news" of every ebb and flow will usually make it more likely that we'll succumb to temptation.

Appendix B

Using the Investorship Calculator

Throughout this book, we have emphasized the potential *multiplier effect* of spending on things that increase in value—specifically low-cost index funds with a predictable, long-term growth rate. To give you a simple way of visualizing that effect, we created an online calculator:

investorship.com/calculator

We recommend that, once you access the calculator, you bookmark it for easy access. Here's what you'll see:

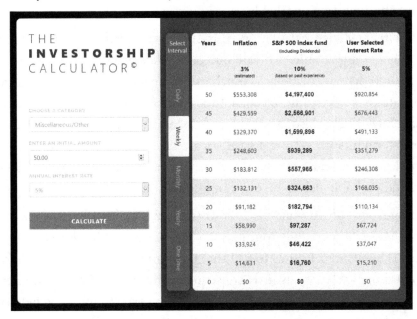

To calculate the multiplier effect, choose a category of spending (optional), enter an initial amount, and an alternate investment yield (also optional). Then choose the spending frequency—daily, weekly, monthly, yearly, or one time, and click "calculate." The calculator will display the totals accrued over certain periods of time, from 5 through 50 years, if that amount were spent differently. The first column is simply the result of doing nothing, assuming the amount of the contribution was adjusted for inflation. The third column is the result of making the

Scan this QR Code with your smartphone or tablet to access the calculator.

same contribution in a "safe" investment, such as a U.S. Treasury note or bond. However, the second column reflects the likely outcome from a low-cost index fund with an average growth rate of 10%, including dividends. As you can see, the long-term results of seemingly small contributions are remarkable.

As with any such calculation, this shows the likely potential result, and is not a guaranteed future outcome. However, while an S&P index fund may fluctuate by as much as 25% in a given year, the historic, long-term growth rate of such funds makes the projected outcome extremely likely. Also, as noted in Appendix A, spending money in a long-term index fund is not an all-or-nothing proposition. Money that you know you must access in the very near future (two years or less) should probably not be invested in a stock fund.

The purpose of this calculator is to provide a reality check when we are making a seemingly routine spending decision. Our *Reactive* (System 1) habits may lead us to feel that paying more than we need to for something we want has little consequence. Our unconscious, momentary response is perfectly normal, but also incorrect. With the help of the calculator, we can engage our *Reflective* (System 2) abilities, objectively knowing the potential long-term forfeiture that such "spilling" entails.

As a practical example, let's assume that a person in their 20s is earning a modest weekly paycheck of $1,000 after taxes. If 3% of that amount is being "spilled" (paying more than is necessary to meet the need or want), then they could instead allocate $30 per week to a low-cost, S&P 500 index fund. By retirement age, the likely end results are impressive:

Comparative projected results of a $30 weekly allocation:

Years	Inflation	S&P 500 Index Fund Including Dividends
	3%	10%
50	$331,985	$2,518,440
45	$257,735	$1,540,140
40	$197,622	$935,937
35	$149,162	$563,573
30	$110,287	$334,779
25	$79,278	$194,797
20	$54,709	$109,676
15	$35,394	$58,372
10	$20,354	$27,853
5	$8,778	$10,056
0	$0	$0

Source: investorship.com/calculator. These estimates represent highly probable results, based on past experience and likely future outcomes, but are not guaranteed.

Of course, the weekly allocation amount can—and should—be increased as their earnings increase. The best way to see the potential, long-term benefit is to use the calculator yourself.

The same formulas apply to monthly, yearly, or one-time contributions. For example, if a professional in their 30s set up an automatic contribution of $300 per month, the likely results would also be impressive:

Comparative projected results of a $300 monthly allocation:

Years	Inflation	S&P 500 Index Fund Including Dividends
	3%	10%
50	$766,119	$5,811,785
45	$594,775	$3,554,171
40	$456,051	$2,159,856
35	$344,220	$1,300,555
30	$254,509	$772,567
25	$182,951	$449,533
20	$126,252	$253,099
15	$81,679	$134,705
10	$46,971	$64,276
5	$20,259	$23,206
0	$0	$0

Source: investorship.com/calculator. These estimates represent highly probable results, based on past experience and likely future outcomes, but are not guaranteed.

Using the Investorship Calculator is not a panacea. You actually have to make the decision to allocate your spending accordingly. As discussed in the book, our normal, Reactive biases are not easy to change. However, by making—and sticking to—a decision to spill less and spend in a normal plus manner, the opportunity to spend your way to wealth can be realized.

Appendix C

Online Resources

The Investorship Calculator is only one part of the website supporting the readers of this book. Following publication, the site will host additional content—including blogs, videos, and other conversations—designed to help the reader explore new ways to address spending and wealth in their daily lives.

To access content on a laptop or desktop computer, just enter the URL:

investorship.com/content

It is not impossible to predict exactly what sorts of "active content" will be available to support the book. Our plan, however, is to include:

Or scan this **QR Code** with your smartphone or tablet to access the website.

- Videos by those known for following the principles identified in this book, including Warren Buffett

- Helpful blogs, vlogs, and podcasts

- Articles that will help you expand your *normal plus* behavior when it comes to spending

- Opportunities to engage with the author—and each other—on social media platforms

We hope you will find these additional materials helpful in your ongoing Investorship journey.

Appendix D

The Forward-Looking Rearview Mirror

Throughout this book, we have stressed how actions in the present will have dramatic but too often unanticipated and adverse effects on future well-being. To ensure our satisfaction in the future, we need to make different decisions *now*. However, in practice, this is easier said than done.

As normal human beings, it's all too easy to focus on the present and ignore or disregard the future. After all, the present is where we actually exist and make choices. Our normal, Reactive (System 1) nature is involved in the majority of those decisions. To conserve effort, we are naturally resistant to exercising our conscious, Reflective (System 2) abilities unless we think it is absolutely necessary. When the future consequences are unclear, we are less likely to consider them. So, when it comes to actions involving spending, we recommend using a technique called *the Forward-Looking Rearview Mirror.*

What a difference a little time makes

Aproximate historic prices.

Rear-View Mirror (RVM)

50 Years Ago	25 Years Ago	
		Average Home
$23,900	$130,000	
		Average Car
$2,500	$12,800	
		Groceries (household)
$1,170	$2,591	
		Big Mac®
$0.65	$1.85	

Forward-Looking RVM

Estimated Prices (at the same rate of increase.)

	In 25 Years *(est.)*	In 50 Years *(est.)*
$331,000 (approximate median price today)	**$842,777**	**$4,584,142**
$37,577 (approximate median price today)	**$110,315**	**$564,812**
$4,363 (approximate average annual spending today)	**$7,347**	**$28,625**
$3.99 (approximate price today)	**$8.61**	**$24.49**

Briefly, this means that by seeing things that have consistently occurred in the past, we can more clearly see what may likely occur in the future. The best example of this mirror technique involves *inflation*.

Without diving into the many theories used to explain monetary inflation, we can all agree that, in general, the price of things have nearly always risen over time. However, mere numbers don't always provide a vivid picture of the past, much less the future.

So, as an example, consider the median price of a home today, which is $331,000. In 1970 (50 years ago), the same median price home was $23,900, and in 1995 (25 years ago), it was $130,000. Taking those same percentage increases, and applying them forward, in 25 years from now, the median home price will be $842,000 and 50 years from now $4,584,000.

As a visual comparison for these numbers, and those of other common expenses, we have created a table on pages 164 and 165. To many, these numbers are alarming—as they should be.

To be sure, our income may keep pace with inflation—or it may not. In either case, sooner or later, that income will cease, as we discussed in Chapter 8. On "Stop Work Day," you will no longer receive income in exchange for your work, and so must find other financial means of meeting your needs.

The Mirror and Investments

Now, apply the Forward-Looking Rearview Mirror concept to investing. Although "past behavior is no guarantee of future performance," as the saying goes, it is still helpful to know what happened historically in order to understand the wisest actions going forward. Take for example the historic returns on what many people consider to be "safe" investments, such as U.S. Government securities. According to Macrotrends, the yield on 10-year U.S. Treasury bonds is relatively stable, although lower than it was 50 and 25 years ago.

Conversely, the annual return rate of the S&P 500 Index has varied widely year-to-year over the same period of time—also according to Macrotrends.

It's important not to be Reactive when looking back at these two, historic indicators, but instead use our Reflective abilities. The steady pace of the "safer" investment *feels* more sensible than the erratic annual returns of the S&P Index. However, in reality, the latter was a far better choice. The *average* return of the S&P 500 has resulted in a consistent increase in price over the same time period—despite occasional, short-term declines:

Now, with an accurate picture in the "Rearview Mirror," apply those averages to your long-term future investments, using the Investorship Calculator:

A modest investment of $100 per month will likely fare far better in the long term with a low-cost S&P 500 index fund than it would with the "safer" alternative—even with a generous bond yield of 4%. Of course, this assumes that the regular, monthly contribution is continued, and that the investor successfully resists the temptation to tinker with the fund, as described in Chapter 8.

Looking back has decided advantages. We cannot change the past, but we can learn from it. It informs us of what prices have been and likely may be in the future. More importantly, it also gives us a better chance of being able to pay those very likely higher prices in the future. It teaches us the best way to allocate today's wealth in a manner that ensures the likelihood of future financial wealth.

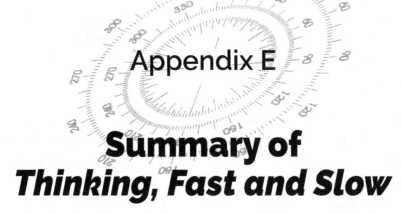

Appendix E

Summary of
Thinking, Fast and Slow

Author's Note: Thinking, Fast and Slow is a best-selling book by Nobel laureate Daniel Kahneman. Published in 2011 by Farrar, Straus and Giroux, it was the 2012 winner of the National Academies Communication Award for best creative work that helps the public understanding of topics in behavioral science, engineering, and medicine.

Thinking, Fast and Slow includes many of the key concepts that were the basis of Kahneman's winning the 2002 Nobel Prize in Economics. He was the only non-economist to ever receive such recognition.

This has been one of many academically sound books that have inspired and aided the author in the writing of *Spending Your Way to Wealth*. A brilliant summary of Kahneman's book has been compiled by Erik Johnson, who has graciously consented to its inclusion here. (All page references in this Appendix are to Kahneman's book.)

Summary by Erik Johnson (used with permission)

Daniel Kahneman's aim in this book is to make psychology, perception, irrationality, decision making, errors of judgment, cognitive science, intuition, statistics, uncertainty, illogical thinking, stock market gambles, and behavioral economics easy for the masses to grasp. Despite his charming and conversational style, this book was difficult for me because I am accustomed to thinking fast. As a service to my fellow automatic, intuitive, error-making, fast thinkers I offer this simple (dumbed down) summary of what is a very helpful book. Writing this summary taught me how to think harder, clearer, and with fewer cognitive illusions. In short, how to think slower. Now if only I'd do it.

INTRODUCTION

This book is about the biases of our intuition. That is, we assume certain things automatically without having thought through them carefully. Kahneman calls those assumptions heuristics (page 7). He spends nearly 500 pages listing example after example of how certain heuristics lead to muddled thinking, giving each a name such as "halo effect," "availability bias," "associative memory," and so forth. In this summary I list Kahneman's heuristics to a list of errors of judgment.

Synonyms for heuristics include "rules of thumb," "presuppositions," "cognitive illusions," "bias of judgment," "thinking errors," "dogmatic assumptions," "systematic errors," "intuitive flaws."

Kahneman did not number his list but I will do so for ease of understanding, citing page numbers as I go. My paragraph summaries are clear, but I of course encourage interested readers to go to the book itself to read up on each heuristic in more detail.

PART ONE: TWO SYSTEMS
CHAPTER 1: THE CHARACTERS OF THE STORY

Our brains are comprised of two characters, one that thinks fast, System 1, and one that thinks slow, System 2. System 1 operates automatically, intuitively, involuntarily, and effortlessly—like when we drive, read an angry facial expression, or recall our age. System 2 requires slowing down, deliberating, solving problems, reasoning, computing, focusing, concentrating, considering other data, and not jumping to quick conclusions—like when we calculate a math problem, choose where to invest money, or fill out a complicated form. These two systems often conflict with one another. System 1 operates on heuristics that may not be accurate. System 2 requires effort evaluating those heuristics and is prone to error. The plot of his book is how to, "recognize situations in which mistakes are likely and try harder to avoid significant mistakes when stakes are high," (page 28).

CHAPTER 2: ATTENTION AND EFFORT

Thinking slow affects our bodies (dilated pupils), attention (limited observation), and energy (depleted resources). Because thinking slow takes work, we are prone to think fast, the path of least resistance. "Laziness is built deep into our nature," (page 35). We think fast to accomplish routine tasks and we need to think slow in order to manage complicated tasks. Thinking fast says, "I need groceries." Thinking slow says, "I will not try to remember what to buy but write myself a shopping list."

CHAPTER 3: THE LAZY CONTROLLER

People on a leisurely stroll will stop walking when asked to complete a difficult mental task. Calculating while walking is an energy drain. This is why being interrupted while concentrating is frustrating, why we forget to eat when focused on an interesting project, why multi-tasking while driving is dangerous, and why resisting temptation is extra hard when we are stressed. Self-control shrinks when we're tired, hungry, or mentally exhausted. Because of this reality we are prone to let System 1 take over intuitively and impulsively. "Most people do not take the trouble to think through [a] problem," (page 45). "Intelligence is not only the ability to reason; it is also the ability to find relevant material in memory and to deploy attention when needed," (page. 46). Accessing memory takes effort but by not doing so we are prone to make mistakes in judgment.

CHAPTER 4: THE ASSOCIATIVE MACHINE

Heuristic #1: PRIMING.

Conscious and subconscious exposure to an idea "primes" us to think about an associated idea. If we've been talking about food, we'll fill in the blank SO_P with a U, but if we've been talking about cleanliness, we'll fill in the blank SO_P with an A. Things outside of our conscious awareness can influence how we think. These subtle influences also affect behavior, "the ideomotor effect," (page 53). People reading about the elderly will unconsciously walk slower. And people who are asked to walk slower will more easily recognize words related to old age. People asked to smile find jokes funnier; people asked to frown find disturbing pictures more disturbing. It is true: if we behave in certain ways our thoughts and emotions will eventually catch up. We can not only feel our way into behavior, we can behave our way into feelings. Potential for error? We are not objective rational thinkers. Things influence our judgment, attitude, and behavior that we are not even aware of.

CHAPTER 5: COGNITIVE EASE

Heuristic #2: COGNITIVE EASE.

Things that are easier to compute, more familiar, and easier to read seem truer than things that require hard thought, are novel, or are hard to see. "Predictable illusions inevitably occur if a judgment is based on the impression of cognitive ease or strain," (page 62). "How do you know that a statement is true? If it is strongly linked by logic or association to other beliefs or preferences you hold, or comes from a source you trust and like, you will feel a sense of cognitive ease," (page 64). Because things that are familiar seem more true teachers, advertisers, marketers, authoritarian tyrants, and even cult leaders repeat their message endlessly. Potential for error? If we hear a lie often enough, we tend to believe it.

CHAPTER 6: NORMS, SURPRISES, AND CAUSES

Heuristic #3: COHERENT STORIES (ASSOCIATIVE COHERENCE).

To make sense of the world we tell ourselves stories about what's going on. We make associations between events, circumstances, and regular occurrences. The more these events fit into our stories the more normal they seem. Things that don't occur as expected take us by surprise. To fit those surprises into our world we tell ourselves new stories to make them fit. We say, "Everything happens for a purpose," "God did it," "That person acted out of character," or "That was so weird it can't be random chance." Abnormalities, anomalies, and incongruities in daily living beg for coherent explanations. Often those explanations involve 1) assuming intention, "It was meant to happen," 2) causality, "They're homeless because they're lazy," or 3) interpreting providence, "There's a divine purpose in everything." "We are evidently ready from birth to have impressions of causality, which do not depend on reasoning about patterns of causation," (page 76). "Your mind is ready and even eager to identify agents, assign them personality traits and specific intentions, and view their actions as expressing individual propensities," (page 76). Potential for error? We posit intention and agency where none exists, we confuse causality with correlation, and we make more out of coincidences than is statistically warranted.

CHAPTER 7: A MACHINE FOR JUMPING TO CONCLUSIONS

Heuristic #4: CONFIRMATION BIAS.

This is the tendency to search for and find confirming evidence for a belief while overlooking counter examples. "Jumping to conclusions is efficient if the conclusions are likely to be correct and the costs of an occasional mistake acceptable, and if the jump saves much time and effort. Jumping to conclusions is risky when the situation is unfamiliar, the stakes are high, and there is no time to collect more information," (page 79). System 1 fills in ambiguity with automatic guesses and interpretations that fit our stories. It rarely considers other interpretations. When System 1 makes a mistake System 2 jumps in to slow us down and consider alternative explanations. "System 1 is gullible and biased to believe, System 2 is in charge of doubting and unbelieving, but System 2 is sometimes busy, and often lazy," (page 81). Potential for error? We are prone to over-estimate the probability of unlikely events (irrational fears) and accept uncritically every suggestion (credulity).

Heuristic #5: THE HALO EFFECT.

"This is the tendency to like or dislike everything about a person—including things you have not observed," (page 82). The warm emotion we feel toward a person, place, or thing predisposes us to like everything about that person, place, or thing. Good first impressions tend to positively color later negative impressions and conversely, negative first impressions can negatively color later positive impressions. The first to speak their opinion in a meeting can "prime" others' opinions. A list of positive adjectives describing a person influences how we interpret negative adjectives that come later in the list. Likewise, negative adjectives listed early color later positive adjectives. The problem with all these examples is that our intuitive judgments are impulsive, not clearly thought through, or critically examined. To remind System 1 to stay objective, to resist jumping to conclusions, and to enlist the evaluative skills of System 2, Kahneman coined the abbreviation, "WYSIATI," what you see is all there is. In other words, do not lean on information based on impressions or intuitions. Stay focused on the hard data before us. Combat over confidence by basing our beliefs not on subjective feelings but critical thinking. Increase clear thinking by giving doubt and ambiguity their day in court.

CHAPTER 8: HOW JUDGMENTS HAPPEN

Heuristic #6: JUDGMENT.

System 1 relies on its intuition, the basic assessments of what's going on inside and outside the mind. It is prone to ignore "sum-like variables," (page 93). We often fail to accurately calculate sums but rely instead on often unreliable intuitive averages. It is prone to "matching," (page 94). We automatically and subconsciously rate the relative merits of a thing by matching dissimilar traits. We are prone to evaluate a decision without distinguishing which variables are most important. This is called the "mental shotgun" approach (page 95). These basic assessments can easily replace the hard work System 2 must do to make judgments.

CHAPTER 9: AN EASIER QUESTION

Heuristic #7: SUBSTITUTION.

When confronted with a perplexing problem, question, or decision, we make life easier for ourselves by answering a substitute, simpler question. Instead of estimating the probability of a certain complex outcome we rely on an estimate of another, less complex outcome. Instead of grappling with the mind-bending philosophical question, "What is happiness?" we answer the easier question, "What is my mood right now?" (page 98). Even though highly anxious people activate System 2 often, obsessing and second guessing every decision, fear, or risk, it is surprising how often System 1 works just fine for them. Even chronic worriers function effortlessly in many areas of life while System 1 is running in the background. They walk, eat, sleep, breath, make choices, make judgments, trust, and engage in enterprises without fear, worry, or anxiety. Why? They replace vexing problems with easier problems. Potential for error? We never get around to answering the harder question.

Heuristic #8: AFFECT.

Emotions influence judgment. "People let their likes and dislikes determine their beliefs about the world," (page 103). Potential for error? We can let our emotional preferences cloud our judgment and either under- or over-estimate risks and benefits.

PART TWO: HEURISTICS AND BIASES

CHAPTER 10: THE LAW OF SMALL NUMBERS

Heuristic #9: THE LAW OF SMALL NUMBERS.

Our brains have a difficult time with statistics. Small samples are more prone to extreme outcomes than large samples, but we tend to lend the outcomes of small samples more credence than statistics warrant. System 1 is impressed with the outcome of small samples but shouldn't be.

Small samples are not representative of large samples. Large samples are more precise. We err when we intuit rather than compute, (see page 113). Potential for error? We make decisions on insufficient data.

Heuristic #10: CONFIDENCE OVER DOUBT.

System 1 suppresses ambiguity and doubt by constructing coherent stories from mere scraps of data. System 2 is our inner skeptic, weighing those stories, doubting them, and suspending judgment. But because disbelief requires lots of work System 2 sometimes fails to do its job and allows us to slide into certainty. We have a bias toward believing. Because our brains are pattern recognition devices, we tend to attribute causality where none exists. Regularities occur at random. A coin flip of 50 heads in a row seems unnatural but if one were to flip a coin billions of times the odds are that 50 heads in a row would eventually happen. "When we detect what appears to be a rule, we quickly reject the idea that the process is truly random," (page 115). Attributing oddities to chance takes work. It's easier to attribute them to some intelligent force in the universe. Kahneman advises, "accept the different outcomes were due to blind luck" (page 116). There are many facts in this world due to change that do not lend themselves to explanations. Potential for error? Making connections where none exists.

CHAPTER 11: ANCHORS

Heuristic #11: THE ANCHORING EFFECT.

This is the subconscious phenomenon of making incorrect estimates due to previously heard quantities. If I say the number 10 and ask you to estimate Gandhi's age at death, you'll give a lower number than if I'd said to you the number 65. People adjust the sound of their stereo volume according to previous "anchors," the parents' anchor is low decibels, the teenager's anchor is high decibels. People feel 35 mph is fast if they've been driving 10 mph but slow if they just got off the freeway doing 65 mph. Buying a house for $200k seems high if the asking price was raised from $180k but low if the asking price was lowered from $220k. A 15-minute wait to be served dinner in a restaurant seems long if the sign in the window says, "Dinner served in 10 minutes or less" but fast if the sign says, "There is a 30-minute wait before dinner will be served." Potential for error? We are more suggestible than we realize.

CHAPTER 12: THE SCIENCE OF AVAILABILITY

Heuristic #12: THE AVAILABILITY HEURISTIC.

When asked to estimate numbers like the frequency of divorces in Hollywood, the number of dangerous plants, or the number of deaths by plane crash, the ease with which we retrieve an answer influences the size of our answer. We're prone to give bigger answers to questions that are easier to retrieve. And answers are easier to retrieve when we have had an emotional personal experience. One who got mugged over-estimates the frequency of muggings, one exposed to news about school shootings over-estimates the number of gun crimes, and the one who does chores at home overestimates the percentage of the housework they do. When both parties assume that they do 70% of the housework somebody is wrong because there's no such thing as 140%! A person who has experienced a tragedy will over-estimate the potential for risk, danger, and a hostile universe. A person untroubled by suffering will under-estimate pending danger. When a friend gets cancer, we get a check-up. When nobody we know gets cancer, we ignore the risk. Potential for error: under or overestimating the frequency of an event based on ease of retrieval rather than statistical calculation.

CHAPTER 13: AVAILABILITY, EMOTION, AND RISK

Heuristic #13: AVAILABILITY CASCADES.

When news stories pile up our statistical senses get warped. A recent plane crash makes us think air travel is more dangerous than car travel. The more we fear air travel the more eager news reporters are to sensationalize plane crashes. A negative feedback loop is set in motion, a cascade of fear. "The emotional tail wags the rational dog," (page 140). Potential for error? Overreacting to a minor problem simply because we hear a disproportionate number of negative news stories to positive ones.

CHAPTER 14: TOM W'S SPECIALTY

Heuristic #14: REPRESENTATIVENESS.

Similar to profiling or stereotyping, "representativeness" is the intuitive leap to make judgments based on how similar something is to something we like without taking into consideration other factors: probability (likelihood), statistics (base rate), or sampling sizes. Baseball scouts used to recruit players based on how close their appearance resembled other good players. Once players were recruited based on actual statistics the level of gamesmanship improved. Just because we like the design of a book cover doesn't mean we'll like the contents. You can't judge a book by its cover. A start-up restaurant has a low chance of survival regardless of how much you like their food. Many well-run companies keep their facilities neat and tidy, but a well-kept lawn is no guarantee that the occupants inside are organized. To discipline our lazy intuition, we must make judgments based on probability and base rates and question our analysis of the evidence used to come up with our assumption in the first place. "Think like a statistician," (page 152). Potential for error: Evaluating a person, place, or thing on how much it resembles something else without taking into account other salient factors.

CHAPTER 15: LINDA: LESS IS MORE

Heuristic #15: THE CONJUNCTION FALLACY (violating the logic of probability).

After hearing priming details about a made-up person (Linda), people chose a plausible story over a probable story. Logically, it is more likely that a person will have one characteristic than two characteristics. That is, after reading a priming description of Linda respondents were more likely to give her two characteristics, which is statistically improbable. It is more likely Linda would be a bank teller (one characteristic) than a bank teller who is a feminist (two characteristics). "The notions of coherence, plausibility, and probability are easily confused by the unwary," (page 159). The more details we add to a description, forecast, or judgment the less likely they are to be probable. Why? Stage 1 thinking overlooks logic in favor of a plausible story. Potential for error: committing a logical fallacy, when our intuition favors what is plausible but improbable over what is implausible and probable.

CHAPTER 16: CAUSES TRUMP STATISTICS

Heuristic #16: OVERLOOKING STATISTICS.

When given purely statistical data we generally make accurate inferences. But when given statistical data and an individual story that explains things, we tend to go with the story rather than statistics. We favor stories with explanatory power over mere data. Potential for error: stereotyping, profiling, and making general inferences from particular cases rather than making particular inferences from general cases.

CHAPTER 17: REGRESSION TO THE MEAN

Heuristic #17: OVERLOOKING LUCK.

Most people love to attach causal interpretations to the fluctuations of random processes. "It is a mathematically inevitable consequence of the fact that luck played a role in the outcome... Not a very satisfactory theory—we would all prefer a causal account—but that is all there is," (page 179). When we remove causal stories and consider mere statistics, we'll observe regularities, what is called the regression to the mean. Those statistical regularities—regression to the mean—are explanations ("things tend to even out") but not causes ("that athlete had a bad day but is now 'hot'). "Our mind is strongly biased toward causal explanations and does not deal well with 'mere statistics,'" (page 182). Potential for error: seeing causes that don't exist.

CHAPTER 18: TAMING INTUITIVE PREDICTIONS

Heuristic #18: INTUITIVE PREDICTIONS.

Conclusions we draw with strong intuition (System 1) feed overconfidence. Just because a thing "feels right" (intuitive) does not make it right. We need System 2 to slow down and examine our intuition, estimate baselines, consider regression to the mean, evaluate the quality of evidence, and so forth. "Extreme predictions and a willingness to predict rare events from weak evidence are both manifestations of System 1. It is natural for the associative machinery to match the extremeness of predictions to the perceived extremeness on which it is based—this is how substitution works," (page 194). Potential for error: unwarranted confidence when we are in fact in error.

PART THREE: OVERCONFIDENCE
CHAPTER 19: ILLUSION OF UNDERSTANDING

Heuristic #19: THE NARRATIVE FALLACY.

In our continuous attempt to make sense of the world we often create flawed explanatory stories of the past that shape our views of the world and expectations of the future. We assign larger roles to talent, stupidity, and intentions than to luck. "Our comforting conviction that the world makes sense rests on a secure foundation: our almost unlimited ability to ignore our ignorance," (page 201). This is most evident when we hear, "I knew that was going to happen!" Which leads to…

Heuristic #20: THE HINDSIGHT ILLUSION.

We think we understand the past, which implies the future should be knowable, but in fact we understand the past less than we believe we do. Our intuitions and premonitions feel truer after the fact. Once an event takes place, we forget what we believed prior to that event, before we changed our minds. Prior to 2008 financial pundits predicted a stock market crash but they did not know it. Knowing means showing something to be true. Prior to 2008 no one could show that a crash was true because it hadn't happened yet. But after it happened their hunches were retooled and became proofs. "The tendency to revise the history of one's beliefs in light of what actually happened produces a robust cognitive illusion," (page 203). Potential for error: "We are prone to blame decision makers for good decisions that worked out badly and to give them too little credit for successful moves that appear obvious only after the fact. When the outcomes are bad, the clients often blame their agents for not seeing the handwriting on the wall—forgetting that it was written in invisible ink that became legible only afterward. Actions that seemed prudent in foresight can look irresponsibly negligent in hindsight," (page 203).

CHAPTER 20: THE ILLUSION OF VALIDITY

Heuristic #21: THE ILLUSION OF VALIDITY.

We sometimes confidently believe our opinions, predictions, and points of view are valid when confidence is unwarranted. Some even cling with confidence to ideas in the face of counter evidence. "Subjective confidence in a judgment is not a reasoned evaluation of the probability that this judgment is correct. Confidence is a feeling, which reflects the coherence of the information and the cognitive ease of processing it" (page 212). Factors that contribute to overconfidence: being dazzled by one's own brilliance, affiliating with like-minded peers, and over valuing our track record of wins and ignoring our losses. Potential for error: Basing the validity of a judgment on the subjective experience of confidence rather than objective facts. Confidence is no measure of accuracy.

CHAPTER 21: INTUITIONS VS. FORMULAS

Heuristic #22: IGNORING ALGORITHMS.

We overlook statistical information and favor our gut feelings. Not good! Forecasting, predicting the future of stocks, diseases, car accidents, and weather should not be influenced by intuition, but they often are. And intuition is often wrong. We do well to consult check lists, statistics, and numerical records and not rely on subjective feelings, hunches, or intuition. Potential for error: "relying on intuitive judgments for important decisions if an algorithm is available that will make fewer mistakes," (page 229).

CHAPTER 22: EXPERT INTUITION: WHEN CAN YOU TRUST IT?

Intuition means knowing something without knowing how we know it. Kahneman's understanding is that intuition is really a matter of recognition, being so familiar with something we arrive at judgments quickly. Chess players "see" the chess board, fire fighters "know" when a building is about to collapse, art dealers "identify" marks of forgeries, parents have a "sixth sense" when their kids are in danger, readers "read" letters and words quickly, and friends "are familiar" with their friends from a distance. Kids become experts at video games, motorists become expert drivers, and chefs become intuitive cooks. How? Recognition—either over long periods of exposure, or quickly in a highly emotional event (accidents). Intuition is immediate pattern recognition, not magic.

Heuristic #23: *TRUSTING EXPERT INTUITION.*

"We are confident when the story we tell ourselves comes easily to mind, with no contradiction and no competing scenario. But ease and coherence do not guarantee that a belief held with confidence is true. The associative machine is set to suppress doubt and to evoke ideas and information that are compatible with the currently dominant story," (page 239). Kahneman is skeptical of experts because they often overlook what they do not know. Kahneman trusts experts when two conditions are met: the expert is in an environment that is sufficiently regular to be predictable and the expert has learned these regularities through prolonged practice. Potential for error: being misled by "experts."

CHAPTER 23: THE OUTSIDE VIEW

Heuristic #24: *THE PLANNING FALLACY*

means taking on a risky project—litigation, war, opening a restaurant—confident of the best-case scenario without seriously considering the worst-case scenario. If we consult others who've engaged in similar projects, we'll get the outside view. Failure to do this increases the potential for failure. Cost overruns, missed deadlines, loss of interest, waning urgency all result from poor planning. Potential for error: "making decisions based on delusional optimism rather than on a rational weight of gains, losses, and probabilities," (page 252). In other words, poorly planned grandiose projects will eventually fail.

CHAPTER 24: THE ENGINE OF CAPITALISM

Heuristic #25: *THE OPTIMISTIC BIAS.*

We are prone to neglect facts, others' failures, and what we don't know in favor of what we know and how skilled we are. We believe the outcome of our achievements lies entirely in our own hands while neglecting the luck factor. We don't appreciate the uncertainty of our environment. We suffer from the illusion of control and neglect to look at the competition (in business start-ups for example). "Experts who acknowledge the full extent of their ignorance may expect to be replaced by more confident competitors, who are better able to gain the trust of clients," (page 263). Being unsure is a sign of weakness so we turn to confident experts who may be wrong. Potential for error: unwarranted optimism which doesn't calculate the odds and therefore could be risky.

PART FOUR: CHOICES
CHAPTER 25: BERNOULLI'S ERRORS

Heuristic #26: OMITTING SUBJECTIVITY.

We often think an object has only intrinsic objective value. A million dollars is worth a million dollars, right? Wrong. Magically making a poor person's portfolio worth a million dollars would be fabulous! Magically making a billionaire's portfolio a worth a million dollars would be agony! One gained, the other lost. Economists have erred by failing to consider a person's psychological state regarding value, risk, anxiety, or happiness. Eighteenth century economist Bernoulli thought money had utility (fixed worth) but he failed to consider a person's reference point. Potential for error: Making decisions on pure logic without considering psychological states.

Heuristic #27: THEORY-INDUCED BLINDNESS.

"Once you have accepted a theory and used it as a tool in your thinking, it is extraordinarily difficult to notice its flaws. If you come upon an observation that does not seem to fit the model, you assume that there must be a perfectly good explanation that you are somehow missing," (page 277). When the blinders fall off the previously believed error seems absurd and the real breakthrough occurs when you can't re-member why you didn't see the obvious. Potential for error: Clinging to old paradigms that have outlived their validity.

CHAPTER 26: PROSPECT THEORY

Kahneman's claim to fame is Prospect Theory (for which he won the Nobel prize in economics). Economists used to believe that the value of money was the sole determinant in explaining why people buy, spend, and gamble the way they do. Prospect Theory changed that by explaining three things: 1) the value of money is less important than the subjective experience of changes in one's wealth. In other words, the loss or gain of $500 is psychologically positive or negative depending on a reference point, how much money one already has. 2) We experience diminished sensitivity to changes in wealth: losing $100 hurts more if you start with $200 than if you start with $1000. And 3) we are loathe to lose money!

Heuristic #28: LOSS AVERSION.

"You just like winning and dislike losing—and you almost certainly dislike losing more than you like winning," (page 281). System 1 thinking compares the psychological benefit of gain with the psychological cost of loss and the fear of loss usually wins. Potential for error: passing by a sure win in order to avoid what we think might be a possible loss even when the odds are in favor of winning.

CHAPTER 27: THE ENDOWMENT EFFECT

Heuristic #29: THE ENDOWMENT EFFECT.

An object we own and use is more valuable to us than an object we don't own and don't use. Such objects are endowed with significance and we're unwilling to part with them for two reasons: we hate loss and it has a history with us. Thus, we won't sell a beloved, useful object unless a buyer offers significant payment. Objects we don't like or don't use sell for less (or we even give them away). Potential for error: Clinging to objects for sentimental reasons at considerable loss of income.

CHAPTER 28: BAD EVENTS

Heuristic #30: LOSS AVERSION.

People will work harder to avoid losses than to achieve gains. Golfers putt for par to avoid bogeys (losing points for going over par) than for birdies (gaining points by putting under par). Contract negotiations stall when one party feels they're making more concessions (losses) than their disputant. People will work harder to avoid pain than to achieve pleasure. Even animals fight more fiercely to maintain territory than to increase territory. Potential for error: underestimating our own and other's attitudes toward loss/gain. They are asymmetrical.

CHAPTER 29: THE FOURFOLD PATTERN

Heuristic #31: THE POSSIBILITY EFFECT.

When highly unlikely outcomes are weighted disproportionately more than they deserve we commit the possibility effect heuristic. Think of buying lottery tickets.

Heuristic #32: THE CERTAINTY EFFECT.

Outcomes that are almost certain are given less weight than their probability justifies. Think of lawyers who offer a "less than perfect" settlement before the trial which would result in an "almost certain victory."

Heuristic #33: THE EXPECTATION PRINCIPLE.

The two heuristics above have this in common: "decision weights that people assign to outcomes are not identical to the probabilities of these outcomes, contrary to the expectation principle" (page 312).

This means people attach values to gains and losses rather than wealth, and decision weights assigned to outcomes are different from probabilities. The fourfold pattern of preferences accounts for this. Potential for error:

People are risk averse when they look at the prospects of a large gain. They'll lock in a sure gain and accept a less than expected value of the gamble.

When the result is extremely large, such as a lottery ticket, the buyer is indifferent to the fact that their chance of winning is extremely small. Without the ticket they cannot win, but with the ticket, they can at least dream.

This explains why people buy insurance. We'll pay insurance because we're buying protection and peace of mind.

This explains why people take desperate gambles. They accept a high probability of just making things worse, for a chance of a slight ray of hope of avoiding the loss they are facing. This type of risk taking can just turn a bad situation into a disaster.

CHAPTER 30: RARE EVENTS

Heuristic #34: OVERESTIMATING THE LIKELIHOOD OF RARE EVENTS.

It makes more sense to pay attention to things that are likely to happen (rain tomorrow) than to things that are unlikely to happen (terrorist attacks, asteroids, terminal illness, floods and landslides). We tend to overestimate the probabilities of unlikely events, and we tend to over-weight the unlikely events in our decisions. This heuristic joins forces with the availability cascade (#13) and cognitive ease (#2) heuristics above. We are more likely to choose the alternative in a decision which is described with explicit vividness, repetition, and relative frequencies (vs. how likely). Potential for error: succumbing to fear mongers who manipulate data in favor of their cause.

CHAPTER 31: RISK POLICIES

Heuristic #35: THINKING NARROWLY.

Most of us are so risk averse we avoid all gambles. This is wrong, says, Kahneman, since some gambles are clearly on our side and by avoiding them, we lose money. One way to decrease risk aversion is to think broadly, looking at the aggregate wins over many small gambles. Thinking narrowly, looking only at short term losses, paralyzes us. But thinking broadly is non-intuitive. It's a System 2 task that takes work. We therefore are wired by System 1 to think irrationally economically (saying no to easy money). The limit of human rationality is so stark Kahneman calls it a "hopeless mirage" (page 335). The ideal of logical consistency is not achievable by our limited minds. Potential for error: passing by risks in our favor.

CHAPTER 32: KEEPING SCORE

Many have a System 1 calculator in their head that "keeps score" not only of the potential financial gains and losses of a transaction but also of the emotional risks, rewards, and possible regrets of our financial decisions. "The emotions that people attach to the state of their mental accounts are not acknowledged in standard economic theory," page 343). Heuristic #36: THE DISPOSITION EFFECT. We are often willing to sell money earning stocks because it makes us feel like wise investors, and less willing to sell losing stocks because it's an admission of defeat. This is irrational since we'd earn more money by selling the losers and clinging to the winners.

Heuristic #37: THE SUNK COST FALLACY.

To avoid feeling bad about cutting our losses and being called a failure, we tend to throw good money after bad, stay too long in abusive marriages, and stay in unhappy careers. This is optimism gone hay-wire.

Heuristic #38: FEAR OF REGRET.

Regret is an emotion we're familiar with and we do well to avoid making decisions that lead to regret. However, we're terrible at predicting how intense those feelings of regret will be. It often hurts less than we think.

CHAPTER 33: REVERSALS

Heuristic #39: IGNORING JOINT EVALUATIONS.

We make decisions differently when asked to make them in isolation than when asked to make them in comparison with other scenarios. For example, a victim in a robbery will be awarded a higher compensation when there are poignant factors involved (the victim was visiting a store he rarely visited) but will be awarded a lower compensation if harmed while in his usual shopping location. When locations are compared (joint evaluation) we realize the victim's location is insignificant and we reverse our original compensation amount. "Joint evaluations highlight a feature that was not noticeable in single evaluations but is recognized as a decisive when detected," (page 359). Potential for error: making decisions in isolation. We should do comparison shopping, compare sentences for crimes, and compare salaries for different jobs. Failure to do so limits our exposure to helpful norms.

CHAPTER 34: FRAMES AND REALITY

Heuristic #40: IGNORING FRAMES.

How a problem is framed determines our choices more than purely rational considerations would imply. More drivers sign the "donate organ" card when they have to check the opt-in box, than drivers who must check the optout box. We are more willing to pay extra for gas when using a credit card (vs. cash) if the fee is framed as "loss of cash discount" than "added credit card surcharge." Doctors prefer interventions where outcomes are a "one-month survival rate of 90%" than to interventions where outcomes are, "10% mortality rate." Both sentences mean the same thing statistically, but the frame of "survival" has greater emotional value than "mortality rates." "The meaning of a sentence is what happens in your associative machinery while you understand it.... In terms of the associations they bring to mind— how System 1 reacts to them—the two sentences really 'mean' different things," (page 363). "Reframing is effortful, and System 2 is lazy," (page 367). Potential for error: Thinking we make decisions in an objective bubble when in fact there are subjective factors at work about which we are unaware.

PART FIVE: TWO SELVES
CHAPTER 35: TWO SELVES

Heuristic #41: IGNORING OUR TWO SELVES.

We each have an "experiencing" self and a "remembering" self. The latter usually takes precedence over the former. That is, I can experience 13 days of vacation bliss but if on the 14th day things go bad I tend to remember the vacation as negative. My memory overrides my experience. Same with a 40-minute blissful record which ends with a scratch. We remember the scratch sound, not the 39 previous minutes of musical enjoyment. "Confusing experience with the memory of it is a compelling cognitive illusion—and it is the substitution that makes us believe a past experience can be ruined. The experiencing self does not have a voice," (page 381).

Heuristic #42: THE PEAK END RULE.

How an experience ends seems to hold greater weight in our memory than how an experience was lived. Similar to the previous heuristic, the peak end rule is shorthand for remembering only how an experience felt at its end not at this worst moment.

Heuristic #43: DURATION NEGLECT.

Another corollary of the two selves: the duration of an unpleasant or pleasant experience doesn't seem to be as important as the memory of how painful or pleasurable the experience was.

CHAPTER 36: LIFE AS HISTORY

Heuristic #44: NARRATIVE WHOLENESS

(my user-friendly name). When we evaluate how well our and others' lives have been lived, we do well to consider the whole narrative and not just the end. But because of the previous three heuristics we are prone to devalue a long, sacrificial, generous life if at the end (or even after death) we discover episodes of selfishness, etc. "A story is about significant events and memorable moments, not about time passing. Duration neglect is normal in a story, and the ending often defines its character" (page 386). Potential for error: paying more attention to longevity than quality, making decisions based on how memorable it will be rather than how exciting and enriching the experience itself will be, and experiencing a moment of pleasure and forfeiting our reputation of integrity.

CHAPTER 37: EXPERIENCED WELL BEING

Heuristic #45: VALUING A REMEMBERING SELF OVER AN EXPERIENCING SELF.

Since most of us rely on unreliable memories we do well to keep in mind what our experiences were like during them, not just at their conclusion. How many of our waking moments are spent in unpleasant emotions or negative states? They are hard to recall! "Our emotional state is largely determined by what we attend to, and we are normally focused on our current activity and immediate environment," (page 394). A person stuck in traffic can still be happy because they're in love, or a person who is grieving may still remain depressed while watching a comedy. Potential for error: not paying attention to what we are doing, letting experiences happen without reflection, and going with the flow with no attempt to alter our schedules, activities, or experiences.

CHAPTER 38: THINKING ABOUT LIFE

Heuristic #46: AFFECTIVE FORECASTING.

Which factor leads to a happier life duration: or experiences? Would a 20-year life with many happy experiences be better than a 60-year life with many terrible experiences? Which would you rather be: happy or old? We are terrible at predicting what will make us happy. When asked the very difficult question, "Overall, how happy is your life?" we substitute an easier question, "How happy am I right now?" (See heuristic #7). "…the responses to global well-being questions should be taken with a grain of salt" (page 399). People make decisions based on what will make them happy in the future but when it's achieved the happiness doesn't last. We don't know our future selves very well.

Heuristic #47: THE FOCUSING ILLUSION.

"Nothing in life is as important as it is when you are thinking about it," (page 402). This means when we're asked to evaluate a decision, life satisfaction, or preference we err if we focus on only one thing. How we answer, "What would make you happy?" depends on many factors and rarely is one factor determinant. Yet folks regularly focus on one issue—income, weather, health, relationships, pollution, etc.—and ignore other important factors. "How much pleasure do you get from your car?" Depends on how much you value the stereo, mileage, looks, age, cost, comfortable seats, tilt of steering wheel, etc. The fact is, our evaluations are often based on the heuristic that while we are thinking of a thing, we generally think better of it, forgetting how infrequently we actually think about those things (income, weather, health, stereo, mileage, looks, etc.) What initially strikes our fancy is absorbed into daily living, we adapt, we acclimate, we experience the initial pleasure less intensely as time progresses. "The remembering self is subject to a massive focusing illusion about the life that the experiencing self endures quite comfortably," (page 406).

Heuristic #48: MISWANTING.

(Daniel Gilbert's phrase). We exaggerate the effect of a significant purchase or changed circumstances on our future well-being. Things that are initially exciting eventually lose their appeal.

CONCLUSIONS

SUMMARY OF THE TWO SELVES.

It's absurd that people willingly choose more pain for longer periods of time that end pleasantly over periods of less pain of shorter duration and end terribly. But such are the powers of heuristics #s 41, 42, 43, and 45.

SUMMARY OF ECONS AND HUMANS.

Kahneman made infrequent mentions of "econs and humans" so I do not emphasize them in my book summary. Here's the gist of his complaint. Economists ("the Chicago school") operate on the assumption that consumers are rational ("internally consistent," "logically coherent," "adhering to rules of logic," page 411) and always will do the rational thing. If not, that's their loss. Kahneman as a behavioral economist of course disagrees and suggests that heuristics influence our choices which are irrational and counter intuitive; we need help making better choices. The Chicago School are libertarians who want government to keep out of the way and let people make their own choices, good or bad (provided they don't hurt others). Economic behaviorists suggest giving people a nudge is sometimes necessary (regulation, writing clearer contracts, truth in advertising, etc.)

SUMMARY OF TWO SYSTEMS.

"This book has described the workings of the mind as an uneasy interaction between two fictitious characters: the automatic System 1 and the effortful System 2," (page 415).

SYSTEM 1	SYSTEM 2
Subconscious values, drives, beliefs that influence our "gut reactions."	Articulates judgments, makes choices, endorses or rationalizes ideas and feelings
Jumps to conclusions regarding causality.	Makes up stories to either confirm or deny those conclusions.
Operates effortlessly.	Requires conscious effort to engage.
Can be wrong but is more often right.	Can be wrong or right depending on how hard it works.
Influenced by heuristics.	Examines those heuristics when so inclined.

"The way to block errors that originate in System 1 is simple in principle: recognize the signs that you are in a cognitive minefield, slow down, and ask for reinforcement from System 2," (page 417).

About the Author

Paul Heys is a tireless advocate for everyday investors—ordinary people who don't have the time, resources, or inclination to understand the specifics of how the financial markets work. (Spoiler alert: Hardly anyone does.) He also has a passionate desire to help those who have not even considered investing. His writing, teaching, and well-received public speaking have inspired many to re-think their "normal" attitudes about spending and wealth.

As a former Air Force officer and flight instructor, Paul learned how to guide others in doing complicated, sometimes tedious things—calmly and thoughtfully. Later, as a founding director of a commercial bank, and as a VP at the international investment firm Smith Barney, he accumulated a wealth of practical insights, which he freely shares in this short volume.

Since the 1990s, Paul has collaborated with University of Washington psychology professor, Dr. Ronald E. Smith, together developing a successful seminar series, Investorship Training™. Based on the principles of behavioral finance pioneered by Nobel Prize-winning psychologist Daniel Kahneman, these seminars help people understand that normal, psychological attitudes and biases are a major factor in making financial investment decisions—sometimes bad ones—and the simple ways to improve them.

Paul lives in Bainbridge Island, Washington, where he works with schools and community organizations to foster greater fiscal literacy.

Endnotes

1   Throughout this book, the use of the term "normal" should always exclude behaviors that can be clinically defined as "abnormal."

2   Reading Kahneman's excellent but nearly 500-page work requires considerable System 2 effort. It is worthwhile, to be sure. However, since that particular challenge may be a bridge too far for many of us, Appendix E of this book provides a brief synopsis.

3   There is ongoing debate and scientific study on how well we can drive while also engaged in various non-driving activities.

4   Mark, Gloria, et al. "The Cost of Interrupted Work: More Speed and Stress." ACM Digital Library, Association for Computing Machinery, Apr. 2008, dl.acm.org/citation.cfm?id=1357072.

5   Roundabouts—even well-designed ones—are not a traffic panacea, especially when it comes to pedestrians. However, among other benefits, they do provide significant improvement in traffic flow.

6   Motion sensors might theoretically work but may not operate correctly with quiet activities such as reading.

7   Some would say giving money away is also a form of spending. Many do it for tax reasons, which directly impacts financial wealth. We can also give away money to meet non-material needs, just to feel good—or less guilty.

8   Beginning in the 1920s, large merchants and airlines had offered charge cards as a convenient means of buying on credit. However, BankAmericard (now Visa) was the first bank-originated, revolving credit system to be accepted by multiple merchants.

9   Secure applications such as Apple Pay, Google Pay, and Samsung Pay use a variety of secure, wireless technologies to transmit credit or debit card information to a vendor at a point-of-purchase location. The user's identity can be verified with techniques such as fingerprint or facial recognition.

10 It is. See Kumar, Yash. "Why Timing or Predicting the Stock Market Is a Futile Exercise." *Aditya Greens*, 17 Feb. 2018, < https://bit.ly/368Nepf >.

11 Very briefly summarized, Kahneman's work holds that people make risk-involved decisions based on the perceived potential value of losses and gains rather than on the final results. These decisions are founded not on optimal,

objectively reasonable outcomes (System 2), but on subjective mental shortcuts (System 1), often focused on only one aspect of a complex problem. According to Kahneman, "the Humans described by prospect theory are guided by the immediate emotional impact of gains and losses, not by long-term prospects of wealth and global utility." (From *Thinking, Fast and Slow*, pp. 286–287.)

12 Statistically, the odds of dying from food poisoning in the U.S. are 1 in 109,067. For falls in the home, they are 1 in 54,533. For vehicular death—by far the riskiest of the three activities—the odds of dying are 1 in 17,625.

13 Simply put, market capitalization is defined as *the total market value* of a company's outstanding shares of stock, calculated by taking the total number of shares multiplied by the share price.

14 Real estate also tends to increase in value, but unless you're planning to move, it's not an asset you can spend on other things.

15 Arguably, experts can handle the explanation part. However, quite often they fail when it comes to predictions.

16 A mutual fund is a professionally managed investment fund that pools money from many investors to purchase securities. Not all mutual funds are the same and some are managed very differently than others.

17 Barber, Brad M., and Terrance Odean. "Trading Is Hazardous to Your Wealth: The Common Stock Investment Performance of Individual Investors." Wiley Online Library, John Wiley & Sons, Ltd, 17 Dec. 2002, onlinelibrary.wiley.com/doi/abs/10.1111/0022-1082.00226.

18 Not all responses to the possibility effect are unreasonable. Buying insurance, for example, is a rational response to the remote probability of a catastrophic event. By sharing part of the responsibility, in the form of deductibles and best practice discounts, insurance policies provide a balanced response to an unknown future.

19 Moskowitz, Clara. "Mind's Limit Found: 4 Things at Once." *LiveScience*. April. 27, 2008.

20 Telis, Gisela, et al. "Multitasking Splits the Brain." *Science*. December 10, 2017.

21 "Median Sales Price for New Houses Sold in the United States." | FRED | St. Louis Federal Reserve, 26 Nov. 2019. <https://bit.ly/2qzHVAg >.

22 "10 Year Treasury Rate - 54 Year Historical Chart." *MacroTrends*, 7 December 2019. < https://bit.ly/368Nepf >.

23 "S&P 500 Historical Annual Returns." *MacroTrends*, 7 December 2019. < https://bit.ly/2YqnnGO >.

Answers to the Questions from Chapter 1

QUESTION 1: The total cost of a bat and a ball is $1.10. The bat costs $1 more than the ball. How much does the ball cost?

ANSWER: Most say ten cents because it seems so obvious: just subtract one number from the other ($1.10 minus $1.00) and you get $0.10. But that's wrong!

Think about the ten-cent answer. If the bat cost one dollar more than a ten-cent ball, then the bat would cost $1.20. But the question started off saying the two together were $1.10. Therefore, the ball cannot cost ten cents. The cost of the ball can be calculated algebraically, but instead just try another number for the cost of the ball. Try *five cents* for example. That would make the bat cost $1.05 (one dollar more than the ball, as stated in the question). Add that $0.05 ball to the $1.05 bat and voilà: $1.10 (the number given in the question).

QUESTION 2: Mary's father has five daughters. The names of the first four daughters are: **Nana, Nene, Nini**, and **Nono**. What's the name of the fifth daughter?

ANSWER: Most people say Nunu, but the correct answer is Mary. As with the previous question, we tend to let our intuition take over making further thought seem unnecessary. Why spend time when the answer seems so obvious? As normal human beings, we tend to spot trends or patterns—and extend them. In this case, the vowels and consonants in the four names led most of us to conclude that the pattern would continue to the next logical combination, Nunu. But the question itself contained the answer: Mary's father's fifth daughter is named Mary.

QUESTION 3: You are a participant in a race on a straight track. You overtake the second person. What position are you in?

ANSWER: Most people say the answer is first place, but the correct answer is second. Again, our affinity for logical patterns and sequences makes it easy jump to the intuitive but incorrect answer. Because "first" precedes "second" we rely on our intuition and fail to calculate what is actually happening in this scenario. If we have only displaced the runner in second place, then we are now in second place and the leader is still ahead.

QUESTION 4: You overtake the last person in the same race. What position are you in?

ANSWER: Most people say, "last place," which is impossible. There can be no answer because no one in a race can be behind the last person in a race. We intuitively jump to the seemingly logical answer, and are disinclined to spend energy unnecessarily, so the easier mental shortcut is often substituted when no correct answer is possible.

QUESTION 5: A person who cannot speak goes into a shop to buy a toothbrush. By imitating the action of brushing his teeth, he successfully expresses his need to the shopkeeper and makes the purchase. Then, a person who is blind comes into the same shop to buy a pair of protective sunglasses. How does she indicate to the shopkeeper what she wants to buy?

ANSWER: Most people say that they imitate the action of putting on sunglasses, which is incorrect. The correct answer is that they ask the storekeeper for a pair of sunglasses!

In the first scenario of the story, the person who could not speak mimed what they wanted. So, we are predisposed to try and make the two stories consistent, rather than slowing down and thinking about what an actual blind individual is capable of doing. They have no speaking impediment, so they just ask.

Don't be frustrated if you answered any of these questions incorrectly. Most people do. In fact, some answer them all incorrectly. Giving the intuitive-but-wrong answer simply proves you have a functioning, System 1-using brain, as we all do.

CPSIA information can be obtained
at www.ICGtesting.com
Printed in the USA
LVHW052113310820
664632LV00017B/304/J